BASICS OF PYTHON

"PYTHON ESSENTIALS: A BEGINNER'S GUIDE FOR CLASS 11 & 12 CBSE"

AADIL KHAN

RUHEEN ALI

"To all those who seek to master the art of Python, May this book ignite your passion for programming, Inspire your creativity in problem-solving, And empower you to build extraordinary things. With dedication and perseverance, May you embark on a journey of endless possibilities, And may Python's elegance and versatility be your guiding light. To the countless lines of code you'll write, And the countless challenges you'll overcome, May this book be your faithful companion, Guiding you through the depths of Python's magic. With boundless curiosity and a thirst for knowledge, May you continue to explore, experiment, and grow, For in the realm of Python, the adventure never ends. This book is dedicated to you, the Python enthusiasts, As you dare to dream and create, may your code transform the world."

Contents

Preface

I am delighted to present this book to you, which has been a labor of love and passion for me. It is the culmination of many years of thinking, writing, and revising, and it represents some of my deepest thoughts and feelings about the world we live in.

Thank you for taking the time to read this book. I am grateful for your attention and your support, and I hope that it brings you joy and enlightenment.

Sincerely,

[Aadil Khan & Ruheen Ali]

Acknowledgements

First and foremost, I want to thank my family, who have always been my greatest cheerleaders. Their love, support, and encouragement have sustained me through the highs and lows of the writing process, and I am lucky to have them in my corner.

And finally, to my readers, who are the reason why I write. Your support, feedback, and engagement have been the driving force behind this book, and I am grateful for your presence in my life.

To all of you, thank you for your generosity, kindness, and belief in me. This book is dedicated to you, and I hope it brings you joy and inspiration.

Sincerely,

[Aadil Khan]

Prologue

Python is a language of immense power and versatility, capable of solving problems and making connections in ways that few other languages can match. It is a language that has taken the world by storm, powering everything from web applications and scientific research to artificial intelligence and data analysis.

This book is an invitation to explore the wonders of Python, to discover its many strengths, and to learn how to use it to solve problems and create new opportunities. Whether you are a seasoned developer looking to expand your skills, or a novice just starting out, this book will guide you through the fundamentals of Python programming, and help you to become a proficient and confident programmer.

In the pages that follow, we will explore the basic syntax and structure of the Python language, and learn how to write programs that can perform a wide range of tasks. We will delve into the world of data structures, algorithms, and object-oriented programming, and discover how to use these tools to build powerful, efficient, and scalable programs.

But more than that, this book is about the joy and excitement of programming. It is about the thrill of seeing an idea come to life in code, and the satisfaction of solving a difficult problem with elegant and efficient code. It is about the satisfaction of mastering a powerful and versatile tool, and the pleasure of creating something new and useful.

So if you are ready to embark on a journey of discovery and exploration, then join me on this adventure into the world of Python programming. Let us discover together the many wonders that this language has to offer, and see where it takes us.

Sincerely,
[Aadil Khan & Ruheen Ali]

ONE
PYTHON-INTRODUCTION

Python is a powerful general-purpose programming language. It is used in web development, data science, creating software prototypes, and so on. Fortunately for beginners, Python has simple easy-to-use syntax. This makes Python an excellent language to learn to program for beginners.

Python is a cross-platform programming language, which means that it can run on multiple platforms like Windows, macOS, Linux, and has even been ported to the Java and .NET virtual machines. **It is free and open-source.**

It was created by **Guido van Rossum** from 1985- to 1990. Like Perl, Python source code is also available under the **GNU General Public License (GPL).** This tutorial gives enough understanding of the Python programming language.

Why Learn Python?

Python is a high-level, interpreted, interactive and object-oriented scripting language. Python is designed to be highly readable.

1. **Easy to Learn and Use**
2. **Expressive Language**
3. **Interpreted Language**
4. **Cross-platform Language**
5. **Free and Open Source**
6. **Object-Oriented Language**

Installing Python

Python distribution is available for a wide variety of platforms. You need to download only the binary code applicable to your platform and install Python.

If the binary code for your platform is not available, you need a C compiler to compile the source code manually. Compiling the source code offers more flexibility in terms of the choice of features that you require in your installation.

Windows Installation

The setting path at Windows

To add the Python directory to the path for a particular session in Windows –

At the command prompt – type path %path%;C:\Python and press Enter.

Note – C:\Python is the path of the Python directory

Python Interpreter

In Python, there are two options/methods for running code:

1. Interactive mode
2. Script mode

Interactive Mode:

An interpreter is a translator in a computer's language which translates the given code line-by-line in machine-readable bytecodes. And if any error is encountered it stops the translation until the error is fixed. Unlike C/C++ etc, Python is an interpreted object-oriented programming language.

The interactive Python shell looks like this:

```
Python 3.10 (64-bit)
Python 3.10.2 (tags/v3.10.2:a58ebcc, Jan 17 2022, 14:12:15) [MSC v.1929 64 bit (AMD64)] on win32
Type "help", "copyright", "credits" or "license" for more information.
>>>
```

Interactive Mode

Python is interactive. When a Python statement is entered and is followed by the Return key, if appropriate, the result will be printed on the screen, immediately, in the next line. This is particularly advantageous in the debugging process. In the interactive mode of operation, Python is used in a similar way as the Unix command line or the terminal.

```
Python 3.10.2 (tags/v3.10.2:a58ebcc, Jan 17 2022, 14:12:15) [MSC v.1929 64 bit (AMD64)] on win32
Type "help", "copyright", "credits" or "license" for more information.
>>> print("Basics Of Python")
Basics Of Python
>>> 2+3
5
>>> print(2+3)
5
>>>
```

Check Output in just next line

```
>>> Name="Concept Classes"
>>> Ch="Search Our YouTube Channel- Concept Study Point"
>>> print(Name + "Subscribe" + Ch)
Concept ClassesSubscribeSearch Our YouTube Channel- Concept Study Point
>>>
```

Script mode in Python

In script mode, anytime we can view the code that we have written inside the file, we can modify it before executing it next time. That's why editing a Python code becomes quite easy in script mode, and we can edit or view the code as many times as we want. We can write long pieces of code with script mode, and that's why many expert programmers prefer it over the interactive mode of execution. The Python file we create using the script mode is usually saved by default inside the folder where our Python IDE is installed, and it is saved with the Python file (".py") extension.

```
Python 3.10.2 (tags/v3.10.2:a58ebcc, Jan 17 2022, 14:12:15) [MSC v.1929
64 bit (AMD64)] on win32
Type "help", "copyright", "credits" or "license()" for more information.
>>>
```

We use IDLE Shell for writing a code

```python
a="Concept"
b="Study"
c="Point"
print("Our YouTube Channel:- "+a+b+c)
```

Input the Code

Output :

```
Python 3.10.2 (tags/v3.10.2:a58ebcc, Jan 17 2022, 14:12:15) [MSC v.1929
64 bit (AMD64)] on win32
Type "help", "copyright", "credits" or "license()" for more information.
>>>
= RESTART: C:/Users/Dell/AppData/Local/Programs/Python/Python310/Book/1.py
Our YouTube Channel:- ConceptStudyPoint
>>>
```

This is the Output of Code

Python Indentation

Indentation refers to the spaces at the beginning of a code line. Where in other programming languages the indentation in code is for readability only, the indentation in Python is very important.

Python uses indentation to indicate a block of code.

```
Python 3.10.2 (tags/v3.10.2:a58ebcc, Jan 17 2022, 14:12:15) [MSC v.1929 64 bit (AMD64)] on
win32
Type "help", "copyright", "credits" or "license()" for more information.
>>>
= RESTART: C:/Users/Dell/AppData/Local/Programs/Python/Python310/Book/Indentation.py
Traceback (most recent call last):
  File "C:/Users/Dell/AppData/Local/Programs/Python/Python310/Book/Indentation.py", line 3
, in <module>
    Print(a+b)
NameError: name 'Print' is not defined. Did you mean: 'print'?
>>>
```

Indentation Example

Python Identifiers

A name in Python is considered to be an identifier, it can be a class name, function name, module name, or a variable name. In Python, we have a set of rules to define these identifiers (names).

```
$ash=1000
print($ash)
```


These are invalid identifiers

   A. The only allowed characters in identifiers:
1. alphabet (lower and upper case)
2. digits (0-9)
3. underscore symbols (_)
   B. Identifiers should not start with digits:
For Example- 10class is not allowed whereas **class10** is allowed
   C. Python Identifiers are case sensitive
Code:
Marks=23

marks=12
print(Marks)
print(marks)
    Output :
23
12

D. Should not use Reserved words

As per the Python document, we have 33 reserved words in Python. We should not be allowed to use these reserved words as identifiers. For example def is a reserved word in Python, we should not use def as an identifier.

Points to note while defining identifiers :

If an identifier starts with _ (underscore) symbol, then it indicates that it is a private identifier.

If an identifier starts with __ (two underscores) symbols, then it indicates that strongly private identifier.

If an identifier starts and ends with __ (two underscores) symbols, then the identifier is a language-defined special name, it is also known as magic methods Example: __add__

Python Keywords

Python has a set of keywords that are reserved words that cannot be used as variable names, function names, or any other identifiers.

There are 33 keywords available in Python. These keywords can't be used as a variable.

True	False	None	and	as
asset	def	class	continue	break
else	finally	elif	del	except
global	for	if	from	import
raise	try	or	return	pass
nonlocal	in	not	is	lambda

Some Keywords in Python

Python Constants

A constant is a type of variable whose value cannot be changed. It is helpful to think of constants as containers that hold information that cannot be changed later.

For Example:

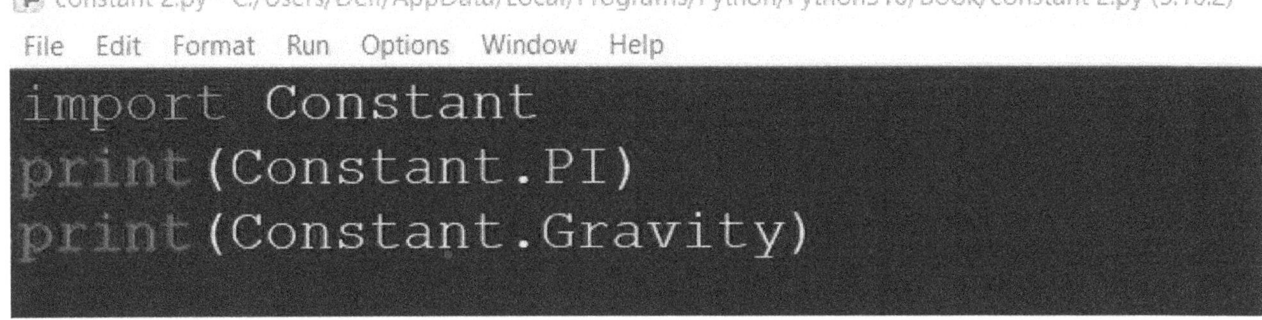

Declared Constant in Constant.py File

First Import keyword is used to import the values

```python
import Constant
print(Constant.PI)
print(Constant.Gravity)
```

Check File Name Properly & Run the Code

Output:
3.14
9.8

Note: In reality, we don't use constants in Python. Naming them in all capital letters is a convention to separate them from variables, however, it does not actually prevent reassignment.

Python Variables

Variables are containers for storing data values. Variable is a name that is used to refer to memory location. Python variable is also known as an identifier and used to hold value. The first character in the variable's name cannot be a number. Variable names can be a group of both the letters and digits, but they have to begin with a letter or an underscore. It is recommended to use lowercase letters for the variable name. Concept and concept are two different variables.

```python
Concept=10 //Declaring Int Variable in python
x="Classes" //Declaring String in python
print(Concept)
print(x)
```

Output:
10
Classes

Casting:

If you want to specify the data type of a variable, this can be done with casting. For Example:

```
    x=str("Concept study point")
print(x)
y=str(3)
print(y)
    Output :
3<class 'str'>
```

TWO
OPERATORS & DATA TYPES

Operators

Operators are special symbols in Python that carry out arithmetic or logical computation. The value that the operator operates on is called the operand. The operator can be defined as a symbol that is responsible for a particular operation between two operands. Operators are the pillars of a program on which the logic is built in a specific programming language.

In Python, we have 7 different types of operators, they are:

1. **Arithmetic Operators**
2. **Comparison Operators**
3. **Assignment Operators**
4. **Logical Operators**
5. **Bitwise Operators**
6. **Membership Operators**
7. **Identity Operators**

1. Arithmetic Operators

Arithmetic operators are used to perform mathematical operations like addition, subtraction, multiplication, etc. Arithmetic operators are used to perform arithmetic operations between two operands. It includes + (addition), - (subtraction), *(multiplication), /(divide), %(reminder), //(floor division), and exponent (**) operators.

```python
x = 20
y = 10
z="Our YouTube Channel - concept Study Point"

print('x + y =',x+y)

print('x - y =',x-y)

print('x * y =',x*y)

print('x / y =',x/y)

print('x // y =',x//y)

print('x ** y =',x**y)

print(z)
```

Arithmetic Operators

Output :

```
x + y = 30
x - y = 10
x * y = 200
x / y = 2.0
x // y = 2
x ** y = 10240000000000
Our YouTube Channel - concept Study Point
```

Output

Floor Division(x//y) – The division of operands where the result is the quotient in which the digits after the decimal point are removed. But if one of the operands is negative, the result is floored, i.e., rounded away from zero(towards negative infinity).

2. *Comparison Operators*

These operators are used to compare the values of operands on either side of this type of operator. These operators return true or false Boolean values. They return true if the condition is satisfied otherwise they return false. Comparison operators are used to comparing values. Comparison Operators are greater than(>), Smaller than(<), Equal to(==), Not Equal to(!=), Greater than or equal to(>=), Less than or equal to (<=).

```
x = 100
y = 120

# Output: x > y is False
print('x > y is',x>y)

# Output: x < y is True
print('x < y is',x<y)

# Output: x == y is False
print('x == y is',x==y)

# Output: x != y is True
print('x != y is',x!=y)

# Output: x >= y is False
print('x >= y is',x>=y)

# Output: x <= y is True
print('x <= y is',x<=y)
```

This is a code using comparison operators

Output:

The output of a code

3. Assignment Operators

The assignment operator is used to assign a specific value to a variable or an operand.

The equal to (=) operator is used to assign a value to an operand directly, if we use an arithmetic operator (+, -, /, etc.) along with the equal to operator then it will perform the arithmetic operation on the given variable and then assign the resulting value to that variable itself.

Let's have a few code examples:

*assignment operators.py - C:/Users/Dell/AppData/Local/Programs/Python/Py

File Edit Format Run Options Window Help

```
x = 5
print(x)
x += 3
print(x)
x -= 3
print(x)
x *= 3
print(x)
x /= 3
print(x)
x %= 3
print(x)
x **= 3
print(x)
x &= 3
print(x)
x ^= 3
```

This is a Code

Output:

```
IDLE Shell 3.10.2
File   Edit   Shell   Debug   Options   Window   Help

Python 3.10.2 (tags/v
AMD64)] on win32
Type "help", "copyrig
>>>

= RESTART: C:/Users/D
  operators.py
5
8
5
15
5.0
2.0
8.0
1
6
>>>
```

Output of Code

4. Logical Operators

The logical operators are used to perform logical operations (like and, or, not) and to combine two or more conditions to provide a specific result i.e. true or false.

In the below code the value of x is true & the value of y is false. When we process "x and y" the output is false because the value of y is false. If one input is false in an operator then output is false. Similarly, we process "x or y" then output is true because in the "OR" operator if one condition is true then output is always true. Similarly, when we process the "Not" operator, the output is false because the Not operator is change the true value to a false value or vice versa.

```
x = True
y = False

print('x and y is',x and y)

print('x or y is',x or y)

print('not x is',not x)
```

Logical Operators Code

Output:
x and y is False
x or y is True
not x is False

5. *Bitwise Operator*

Bitwise operator acts on the operands bit by bit. These operators take one or two operands. Some of the bitwise operators appear to be similar to logical operators but they aren't. The bitwise operators perform bit by bit operation on the values of the two operands. Bitwise Operator are :

& : Bitwise AND - If both the bits at the same place in two operands are 1, then 1 is copied to the result. Otherwise, 0 is copied.

| : Bitwise OR- The resulting bit will be 0 if both the bits are zero; otherwise, the resulting bit will be 1.

~ : Bitwise NOT -It calculates the negation of each bit of the operand, i.e., if the bit is 0, the resulting bit will be 1 and vice versa.

^ : Bitwise XOR - The resulting bit will be 1 if both the bits are different; otherwise, the resulting bit will be 0.

>> : Bitwise right shift - The left operand is moved right by the number of bits present in the right operand.

<< : Bitwise left shift - The left operand value is moved left by the number of bits present in the right operand.

```
x=5
y=3
print('x&y : ', x&y)
print('x|y : ', x|y)
print('~x : ', ~x)
print('x^y : ', x^y)
print('x>>2 : ', x>>2)
print('x<<2 : ', x<<2)
```

Bitwise Operators

Output :

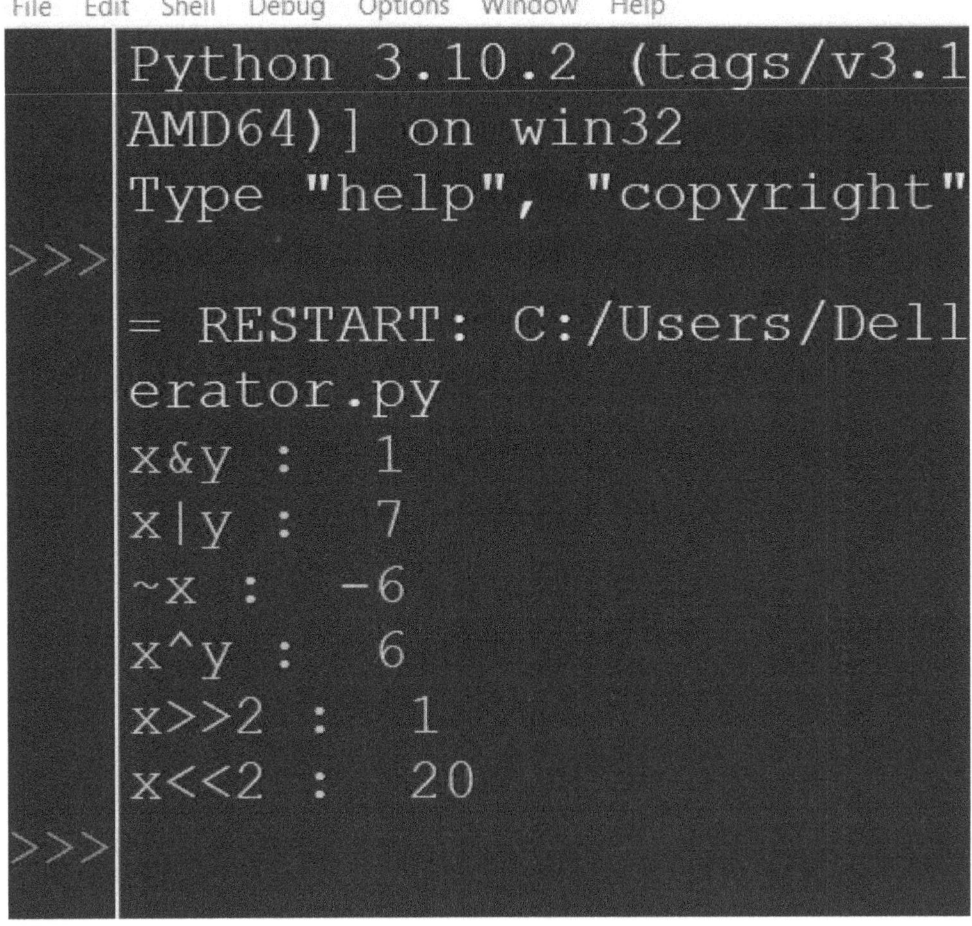

Output

6. Membership Operators

Membership operators are used to searching for a particular element in a string, list, tuple, set Etc.,

    in: Returns True - if the value of the variable is found in the sequence.

    not in: Returns True - if the value of the variable is not found in the sequence.

```
num=[1,2,3,4,5,6]
f="Concept Study Point"
x=3
y="classes"
print(x not in num)
print(y in f)
```

Membership Operator

Output:
FALSE
TRUE

7. Identity Operator

The identity operators are used to test whether a variable refers to the same value/object or not. It returns True or False as output. Identity operators are used to comparing the address of the memory locations which are pointed by the operands. Identity operators return True or False.

is: Returns True - if two operands are identical (refers to the same object).

is not: Returns True - True if operands are not identical (do not refer to the same object).

Code:
x="Concept"
y="Classes"
print(x is not y)
print(x is y)
Output:
True
False

Data Types in Python

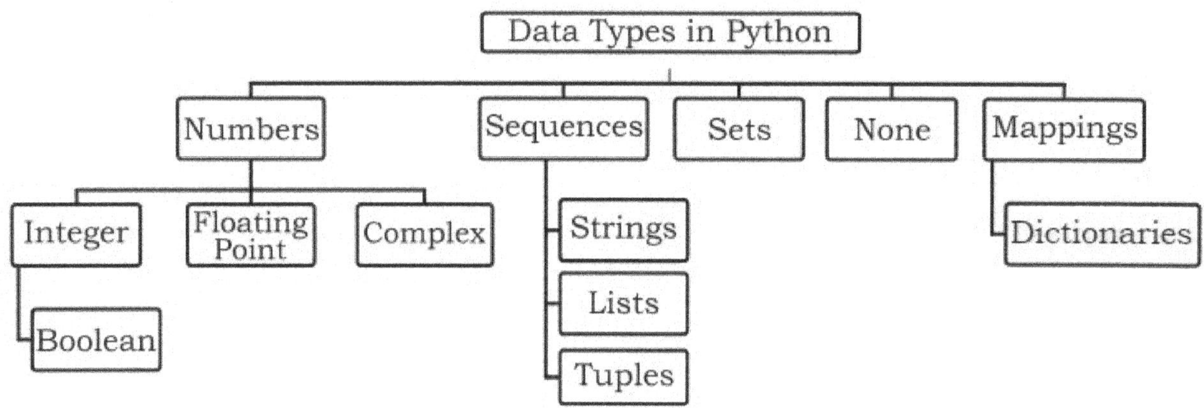

Data Types in Python

First, let's understand what Data Types are? As the name itself suggests, these are some different types of data that the python compiler understands. Just like the Computer can understand only binary numbers (i.e., 1 and 0), that is the one and only data type that a Computer can understand but python has more. As far as Python, programmers are provided with various ways of representing data - like your name, roll number, marks, to the height of Mt. Everest, world population, etc. Basically, anything that holds some raw information.

Data Type represents a type of data present in a variable.

Python supports the following inbuilt data types :

1. int
2. float
3. complex
4. bool
5. str
6. bytes
7. bytearray
8. range
9. list
10. tuple
11. set
12. frozenset
13. dict
14. None

Python enables us to check the type of variable used in the program. Python provides us with the **type() function**, which returns the type of the variable passed.

Code:

```
a=4
print(type(a))
a="Concept"
print(type(a))
a=12.5
print(type(a))
```

```
a=10+5j
print(type(a))
a=True
print(type(a))
a=[1,2,3,4,5]
print(type(a))
    Output:
<class 'int'>
<class 'str'>
<class 'float'>
<class 'complex'>
<class 'bool'>
<class 'list'>
```

String

It is an ordered sequence of letters/characters. They are enclosed in single quotes (' ') or double quotes (" ").

Lists

It is also a sequence of values of any type. Values in the list are called elements/items. Lists are mutable and indexed/ordered. The list is enclosed in square brackets [ ].

Tuples

They are a sequence of values of any type and are indexed by integers. Tuples are enclosed in curved brackets i.e., (). Tuples are also pretty much like Lists, except that they are immutable, hence once we assign it some value, we cannot change it later. At the same time, it is faster in implementation than List.

Examples

```
a=4
print(type(a))
a="Concept"
print(type(a))
a=12.5
print(type(a))
a=10+5j
print(type(a))
a=True
print(type(a))
a=[1,2,3,4,5]
print(type(a))
a=("hi",2,"1")
print(type(a))
    Output:
    <class 'int'>
<class 'str'>
```

<class ‘float’>
<class ‘complex’>
<class ‘bool’>
<class ‘list’>
<class ’tuple'>

Mapping

Mapping is an unordered data type in Python. Currently, there is only one standard mapping data type in python called Dictionary.

Dictionary

Dictionary in Python is an unordered collection of data values, used to store data values like a map, which, unlike other Data Types that hold only a single value as an element, Dictionary holds key:value pair.

dictionary.py - C:/Users/Dell/AppData/Local/Programs/Python/Python310/Book/dictionary.py (3.10.2)
File Edit Format Run Options Window Help

```
Dict = {1: 'Concept', 2: 'Study', 3: 'Point'}
print("\nDictionary with the use of Integer Keys: ")
print(Dict)
Dict1 = {'Name': 'Concept Classes', 1: [1, 2, 3, 4]}
print("\nDictionary with the use of Mixed Keys: ")
print(Dict1)
Dict[4]='our youtube channel' #Adding new element in Dictionary
print(Dict)
```

Code for Dictionary

IDLE Shell 3.10.2
File Edit Shell Debug Options Window Help

```
Python 3.10.2 (tags/v3.10.2:a58ebcc, Jan 17 2022, 14:12:15) [MSC v.1
AMD64)] on win32
Type "help", "copyright", "credits" or "license()" for more informat
>>>
= RESTART: C:/Users/Dell/AppData/Local/Programs/Python/Python310/Boo
.py

Dictionary with the use of Integer Keys:
{1: 'Concept', 2: 'Study', 3: 'Point'}

Dictionary with the use of Mixed Keys:
{'Name': 'Concept Classes', 1: [1, 2, 3, 4]}
{1: 'Concept', 2: 'Study', 3: 'Point', 4: 'our youtube channel'}
>>>
```

Output Dictionary

Sequences DataTypes in Python:

1. Strings: Strings are sequences of characters. They are immutable, meaning their contents cannot be changed after they are created.
Code:
my_string = "Hello, World!"
Output:
Hello, World!

2. Tuples: Tuples are similar to lists, but they are immutable, meaning once created, their elements cannot be changed. They are often used for representing fixed sets of values.
Code:
my_tuple = (1, 2, 3, 4, 5)
print(my_tuple)
Output:
(1, 2, 3, 4, 5)
3. Lists: Lists are ordered collections of elements, and they can contain a mix of different types. Lists are mutable, so you can add, remove, and modify elements.
Code:
my_list = [1, 2, 3, 4, 5]
print(my_list)
Output:
[1, 2, 3, 4, 5]
Range Objects: Range objects represent a sequence of numbers. They are often used for iterating over a sequence of numbers in a for loop.
Code:
my_range = range(1, 6) # Creates a range from 1 to 5
print(list(my_range))
Output
[1, 2, 3, 4, 5]
Python provides various methods and functions for working with sequences, allowing you to perform operations like indexing, slicing, iterating, and more. Here are some common operations:
1. Indexing and Slicing:
Indexing and slicing are fundamental operations for working with sequences in Python. These operations are commonly used with strings, lists, tuples, and other sequence types to access specific elements or subranges within the sequence.
Indexing allows you to access individual elements of a sequence by specifying their position using an index. In Python, indexing starts at 0 for the first element, -1 for the last element, and so on.
Code:
my_list = [10, 20, 30, 40, 50]
print(my_list[0]) # Accesses the first element (10)
print(my_list[2]) # Accesses the third element (30)
print(my_list[-1]) # Accesses the last element (50)
Output:
10
30
50

Slicing:

Slicing allows you to extract a portion (subsequence) of a sequence by specifying a range of indices. The syntax for slicing is [start:stop:step], where start is the index of the first element to include, stop is the index of the first element to exclude, and step is the interval between elements.

Code:

```python
my_list = [10, 20, 30, 40, 50]
print(my_list[1:4]) # Slices from index 1 to 3: [20, 30, 40]
print(my_list[:3]) # Slices from beginning to index 2: [10, 20, 30]
print(my_list[2:]) # Slices from index 2 to the end: [30, 40, 50]
print(my_list[::2]) # Slices with step 2: [10, 30, 50]
print(my_list[::-1]) # Reverses the list: [50, 40, 30, 20, 10]
```

Output:

```
[20, 30, 40]
[10, 20, 30]
[30, 40, 50]
[10, 30, 50]
[50, 40, 30, 20, 10]
```

2. Iterating: Iterating in Python involves traversing or looping through the elements of a sequence, such as a list, tuple, string, or other iterable objects. Iteration is a fundamental concept in programming that allows you to perform actions on each element in a sequence.

Code:

```python
my_tuple = (1, 2, 3, 4, 5)
for item in my_tuple:
print(item)
```

Output:

```
1
2
3
4
5
```

3. Concatenation and Repetition:

Concatenation and repetition are operations that can be performed on sequences in Python, such as strings, lists, and tuples.

Concatenation: Concatenation involves combining two or more sequences to create a new sequence. The + operator is used for concatenation.

Code:

```python
# Concatenation of two lists
list1 = [1, 2, 3]
list2 = [4, 5, 6]
result_list = list1 + list2
print(result_list) # Output: [1, 2, 3, 4, 5, 6]
    # Concatenation of two strings
string1 = "Concept"
string2 = "Classes"
result_string = string1 + " " + string2
print(result_string)
```

Output:

```
"Concept Classes"
```

THREE

INPUT & OUTPUT

Expression

A Python program contains one or more statements. A statement contains zero or more expressions. Python executes a statement by evaluating its expressions to values one by one.

An expression is defined as a combination of constants, variables, and operators. An expression always evaluates a value. A value or a standalone variable is also considered as an expression but a standalone operator is not an expression. Some examples of valid expressions are given below.

(i) num – 20.4

(ii) 3.0 + 3.14

(iii) 23/3 -5 * 7(14 -2)

(iv) "Concept"+"Classes"

Precedence of Operators

The higher precedence operator is evaluated before the lower precedence operator. In the following example, '*' and '/' have higher precedence than '+' and '-'

a) Parenthesis can be used to override the precedence of operators. The expression within () is evaluated first.

b) For operators with equal precedence, the expression is evaluated from left to right.

For Example:

1. How will Python evaluate the following expression?

20 + 10 * 30

precedence of * is more than that of +

= 20+300

= 320

2. How will Python evaluate the following expression?

(20 + 30) * 40

using parenthesis(), we have forced precedence of + to be more than that of *

= 50*40

= 2000

3. How will the following expression be evaluated?

15.0 / 4.0 + (8 + 3.0)

= 15.0/4.0+(11.0)

= 3.75 +11.0

= 14.75

In Python, expressions are combinations of values, variables, and operators that can be evaluated to produce a result. When an expression is evaluated, the operators are applied to the operands (values or variables) according to their precedence and associativity, resulting in a final value. Let's look at some examples of expression evaluation:

Code :

```python
# Exponentiation and Multiplication
result = 2 + 3 ** 2
print(result) # Output: 11
    # Multiplication and Addition
result = 2 * 3 + 4
print(result) # Output: 10
    # Parentheses to Override Precedence
result = (2 + 3) * 4
print(result) # Output: 20
    # Comparison Operators
x = 5
y = 3
result = x > y and x != y
print(result) # Output: True
    # Logical Operators
a = True
b = False
c = True
result = a or b and c
print(result) # Output: True
    # Bitwise Operators
x = 5
y = 3
result = x | y & x
print(result) # Output: 5
    # Assignment Operators
x = 10
x += 5
print(x) # Output: 15
```

These examples illustrate how the precedence of operators affects the evaluation of expressions in Python. Remember that when in doubt about the order of evaluation, using parentheses can help make the desired order explicit and avoid potential confusion.

InPut and outPut

In Python, we have the input() function for taking values entered by input devices such as a keyboard. The input() function prompts the user to enter data. It accepts all user input (whether alphabets, numbers or special characters) as strings. The syntax for input() is:

variable = input([Prompt])

Prompt is the string we may like to display on the screen prior to taking the input, but it is optional.

Code:

```python
    a=input("Enter Name")
print(a)
b=float(input("Enter age"))
```

print(b)
   Output:
   Enter Name Concept Classes
Concept Classes
Enter age 24
24

DebuggIng

Due to errors, a program may not execute or may generate the wrong output.

Errors are problems in a program due to which the program will stop the execution. On the other hand, exceptions are raised when some internal events occur which change the normal flow of the program.

Two types of Errors occur in Python.

1. **Syntax errors**
2. **Logical errors (Exceptions)**

Syntax Errors

When the proper syntax of the language is not followed then a syntax error is thrown. Python has rules that determine how a program is to be written. This is called syntax. The interpreter can interpret a statement of a program only if it is syntactically correct.

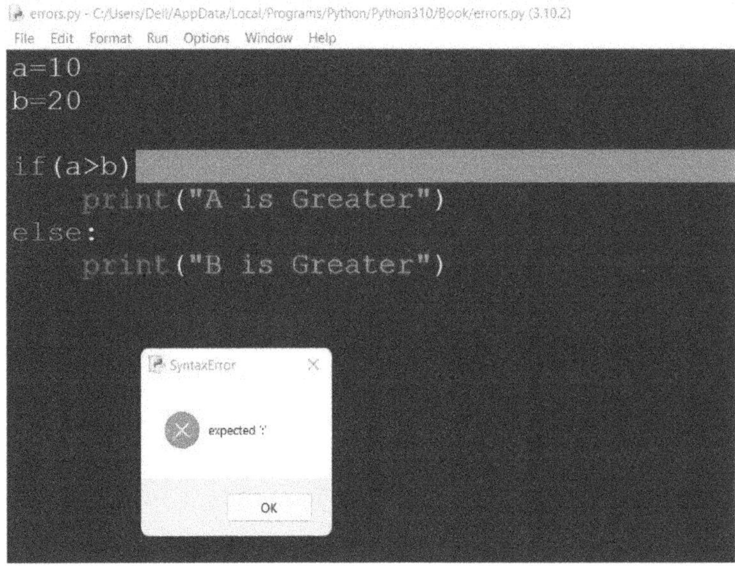

Syntax Error

A syntax error in Python occurs when the code violates the language's rules for proper structure and formatting. These errors prevent the Python interpreter from parsing and understanding the code, leading to a traceback with an error message. Some common causes of syntax errors include:

1. Misspelled Keywords or Identifiers:

Using incorrect spellings for Python keywords, such as "if" instead of "elif" or "def" instead of "dfe." Typo in variable or function names, such as using "printt" instead of "print."

2. Missing or Mismatched Parentheses, Brackets, or Braces:
Forgetting to close parentheses, brackets, or braces.
Mixing different types of brackets, like using [ ] instead of { } for dictionaries.
3. Indentation Errors:
Incorrect indentation levels, such as using spaces instead of tabs or vice versa.
Inconsistent indentation within a block of code, such as an if statement or a loop.
4. Missing Colons:
Forgetting to include a colon : after a statement that requires one, like in if, else, elif, for, while, or def blocks.
5. Invalid Operators:
Using invalid operators or incorrect combinations of operators.
6. Unmatched Quotes:
Not properly closing a string with matching single or double quotes.
Code:

```python
# Example 1: Misspelled keyword
for i in range(5)
print(i)
    # Example 2: Missing colon
if x > 10
print("x is greater than 10")
    # Example 3: Unmatched quotes
message = 'Hello, world!"
    # Example 4: Invalid operator
result = 10 ++ 5
    # Example 5: Incorrect indentation
if condition:
print("Indentation error")
    # Example 6: Missing closing parenthesis
print("Syntax error"
    # Example 7: Inconsistent indentation
for i in range(5):
print(i)
print(i+1) # Indentation should be consistent with the previous line
```

Logical Errors

A logical error/bug (called semantic error) does not stop execution but the program behaves incorrectly and produces undesired /wrong output. Since the program interprets successfully even when logical errors are present in it, it is sometimes difficult to identify these errors.

A logical error in Python, also known as a semantic error, occurs when the code runs without raising any syntax or runtime errors, but it produces incorrect or unexpected results due to flawed logic or incorrect algorithmic implementation. Unlike syntax errors, logical errors are harder to identify since the code itself is valid, but the output does not meet the intended logic. Debugging logical errors often requires careful inspection and understanding of the code's intended behavior. Some common causes of logical errors include:
1. Incorrect Mathematical Operations:
Using the wrong arithmetic operator, such as addition instead of multiplication, leading to incorrect calculations.
2. Wrong Conditional Statements:
Using incorrect logic in conditional statements, leading to incorrect branching or not entering the correct branch.
3. Off-by-One Errors:

Incorrectly iterating through lists or arrays, resulting in skipping or accessing elements outside the intended range.

4. Misunderstanding of Loop Conditions:

Incorrect loop conditions leading to underflow or overflow, causing the loop to execute incorrectly.

5. Incorrect Function Logic:

Functions not returning the expected results due to improper calculations or incorrect algorithmic design.

6. Misuse of Logical Operators:

Using logical operators (and, or, not) incorrectly, leading to unintended behavior of conditional expressions.

Runtime Error

A runtime error causes abnormal termination of program while it is executing. Runtime error is when the statement is correct syntactically, but the interpreter can not execute it. The process of identifying and removing logical errors and runtime errors is called debugging. We need to debug a program so that is can run successfully and generate the desired output.

Comments in python

In Python, comments are used to add explanatory notes or annotations to your code that are ignored by the interpreter. They help improve code readability and understanding, both for yourself and for others who might read your code. Python supports two types of comments:

1. Single-line comments: These comments are used for adding explanations to a single line of code. They start with the # symbol and continue until the end of the line.

2. Multi-line comments (docstrings): While not exactly traditional multi-line comments, Python uses multi-line strings (known as docstrings) for documentation purposes. They are often used to provide detailed explanations of classes, functions, or modules. Docstrings are enclosed in triple quotes (''' or """) and can span multiple lines.

Code :

```
"""
This is a multi-line comment (docstring) that can span
across multiple lines. It's often used to document functions
or classes.
"""
print("Subscribe Our Youtube Channel- Concept Study Point")
```

Output:

Subscribe Our Youtube Channel- Concept Study Point

Explicit Conversion :

Explicit type conversion, also known as type casting or type coercion, involves manually converting a value from one data type to another in a programming language. This is typically done using built-in functions or methods provided by the language. The purpose of explicit type conversion is to ensure that operations involving different data types are performed as intended.

In explicit type conversion, you, as the programmer, take control of the conversion process, indicating the desired data type for the value. Here's a theoretical overview of explicit type conversion:

Why Explicit Type Conversion?

Different data types have different representations and behaviors. When you perform operations involving different data types, the programming language needs to handle how the values interact. Explicit type conversion allows you to specify how you want these interactions to occur.

Common Conversion Functions: Most programming languages provide functions or methods to explicitly convert values between different data types. These functions ensure that the value is properly transformed without unexpected behavior.

1. **int(value): Converts a value to an integer.**
2. **float(value): Converts a value to a floating-point number.**
3. **str(value): Converts a value to a string.**
4. **list(value), tuple(value), set(value), dict(value): Converts between collection types.**

...and more, depending on the language.

Code:

```
# Converting to Integer
float_num = 3.14
int_num = int(float_num)
print("Converting to Integer:", int_num) # Output: 3
    # Converting to Float
int_num = 5
float_num = float(int_num)
print("Converting to Float:", float_num) # Output: 5.0
    # Converting to String
number = 42
string_number = str(number)
print("Converting to String:", string_number) # Output: "42"
    # Converting between Collection Types
my_list = [1, 2, 3]
my_tuple = tuple(my_list)
print("Converting List to Tuple:", my_tuple) # Output: (1, 2, 3)
    # Handling Conversion Errors
string_value = "abc"
try:
int_from_string = int(string_value) # Raises a ValueError
except ValueError:
print("Conversion failed")
    Output:
Converting to Integer: 3
Converting to Float: 5.0
Converting to String: 42
Converting List to Tuple: (1, 2, 3)
Conversion failed
```

Implicit Conversion :

Implicit type conversion, also known as type coercion, is the automatic conversion of values from one data type to another by the programming language itself. This occurs when an operation involves operands of different data types. Python performs implicit type conversions to ensure that the operation can be carried out without errors and with meaningful results.

Why Implicit Type Conversion?

Implicit type conversion is used to facilitate operations between different data types without requiring the programmer to manually perform type casting. It aims to make code more flexible and intuitive by allowing different data types to interact in expressions.

Code:

```python
# Implicit Conversion in Arithmetic Operations
int_num = 5
float_num = 3.14
result = int_num + float_num # Implicit conversion of int to float
print("Arithmetic Result:", result) # Output: 8.14
    # Implicit Conversion in Comparisons
x = 5
y = 5.0
result = x == y # Implicit conversion of int to float
print("Comparison Result:", result) # Output: True
    # Implicit Conversion in Boolean Evaluations
x = 10
if x: # Implicit conversion of int to boolean
print("x is not zero") # Output: "x is not zero"
    # Implicit Conversion with Different Data Types
num = 42
string_num = "42"
result = num == string_num # Implicit conversion of int to string
print("Comparison Result:", result) # Output: True
    Output:
Arithmetic Result: 8.14
Comparison Result: True
x is not zero
Comparison Result: False
```

FOUR
CONTROL STATEMENTS & LIST

Control Statements

1. *if Statements*

if statement is the most simple decision-making statement. It is used to decide whether a certain statement or block of statements will be executed or not i.e if a certain condition is true then a block of statement is executed otherwise not.

SYNTAX:

if condition:

\# Statements to execute if

\# condition is true

```
a=int (input("Enter a Number: "))
if(a>10):
    print("The number is greater than 10: ",a)
```

Code

Output:

```
Python 3.10.2 (tags/v3.10.2:a58ebcc,
AMD64)] on win32
Type "help", "copyright", "credits" o

>>>
= RESTART: C:/Users/Dell/AppData/Loca
ts.py
Enter a Number: 15
The number is greater than 10:  15
>>>
```

Output

2. *if-else*

There are two more keywords that are optional but can be accompanied with if statements, the are:
1. else
2. elif (also known as else if)
The if statement alone tells us that if a condition is true it will execute a block of statements and if the condition is false it won't. But what if we want to do something else if the condition is false. Here comes the else statement. We can use the else statement with if statement to execute a block of code when the condition is false.
Syntax :
if condition:
#block of statements
else:
#another block of statements (else-block)
Code:

```
a=int (input("Enter I Number: "))
b=int (input("Enter II Number: "))
if(a>b):
print("The I number is Greater : ",a)
else:
print("The II Number is Greater : ",b)
```

Output:
Enter I Number: 67
Enter II Number: 34
The I number is Greater : 67

3. *The elif condition*

Syntax
if[condition #1]:
[statement #1]

```
elif[condition #2]:
[statement #2]
elif[condition #3]:
[statement #3]
```

Code :

```
#Concept Study Point is our YouTube Channel
a=int (input("Enter I Number: "))
b=int (input("Enter II Number: "))
c=int (input("Enter III Number: "))
if(a>b & a>c):
print("The I number is Greater : ",a)
elif(b>a & b>c):
print("The II Number is Greater : ",b)
else:
print("The III Number is Greater : ",c)
```

Indentation in Python :

In Python, indentation plays a crucial role in defining the structure and scope of your code. Unlike many other programming languages that use braces {} or keywords like begin and end to define code blocks, Python uses indentation to indicate blocks of code. This is one of the distinctive features of the language and helps in maintaining a clean and readable code style.

Here's how indentation works in Python:

Block Structure: Code blocks in Python are defined by the level of indentation. Indenting code lines creates a block, and dedenting (moving back to the previous level of indentation) indicates the end of a block.

Consistent Indentation: All lines within a single block must have the same level of indentation. This consistency is crucial for Python to understand the structure of your code.

Spaces or Tabs: While you can use either spaces or tabs for indentation, it's recommended to be consistent throughout your codebase. Most Python style guides recommend using 4 spaces for each level of indentation.

No Curly Braces: Unlike languages like C++, Java, or JavaScript, Python does not use curly braces {} to define code blocks. Indentation is the sole indicator of block structure.

Here's an example of how indentation is used in Python:

Code:

```
def greet(name):
if name:
print(f"Hello, {name}!")
else:
print("Hello, stranger!")
    # Function call
greet("Alice")
greet("Bob")
```

Output:

In the example above, the if and else blocks are indented, indicating that they are part of the greet function. The function calls are not indented, showing that they are outside the function.

ррр

Basic of List in Python

List in Python

There are four collection data types in the Python programming language:
1. **List** is a collection that is ordered and changeable. Allows duplicate members.
2. **Tuple** is a collection that is ordered and unchangeable. Allows duplicate members.
3. **Set** is a collection that is unordered, unchangeable, and unindexed. No duplicate members.
4. **Dictionary** is a collection that is ordered and changeable. No duplicate members.

A list in Python is used to store the sequence of various types of data. Python lists are the mutable type which means we can modify its element after it is created. The values that make up a list are called its elements, and they can be of any type. The elements in a list are indexed according to a definite sequence and the indexing of a list is done with 0 being the first index. Each element in the list has its definite place in the list, which allows duplicating of elements in the list, with each element having its own distinct place and credibility.

Creating list

Lists in Python can be created by just placing the sequence inside the **square brackets[]**. The items in the list are separated with the comma (,)

Code

```
#Just Search us on YouTube- "CONCEPT STUDY POINT"
emp = ["Concept Classes", 1001, "Jaipur"] //String & Integer value are declared
Dep1 = ["CS",10]
Dep2 = ["IT",11]
print("Emp Data")
print("Name : %s, ID: %d, City: %s"%(emp[0],emp[1],emp[2]))
print("Department Details")
print("Department : %s, \tDep_ID: %d"%(Dep1[0],Dep1[1]))
```

Output

Name : Concept Classes, ID: 1001, City: Jaipur
Department Details
Department : CS, Dep_ID: 10

List Length

To determine how many items a list has, use the len() function:

Code:

```
#Just Search us on YouTube- "CONCEPT STUDY POINT"
emp = ["Concept Classes", 1001, "Jaipur"]
print(len(emp))
```

Output:

3

Append()

This function adds the element/elements as a single entity to the end of the list. Be it a single element, a list, or a string, it will only add a single entity at the end of the list. In case you want to use this function to add elements in a new list to an existing list, then the new list will be added as a list only.

Code :
```
#Just Search us on YouTube- "CONCEPT STUDY POINT"
emp = ["Concept Classes", 1001, "Jaipur"]
emp.append("Rajasthan")
print(emp)
```
Output :
['Concept Classes', 1001, 'Jaipur', 'Rajasthan']

extend()

When you wish to append multiple items to a list and the goal is to store them as separate entities/elements, use the extend function. extend(), this method is used to add multiple elements at the same time at the end of the list.

Code :
```
emp = ["Concept Classes", 1001, "Jaipur"]
emp.append("Rajasthan")
emp.extend(["Our Book is Launched",3])
print(emp)
```
Output :
['Concept Classes', 1001, 'Jaipur', 'Rajasthan', 'Our Book is Launched', 3]

insert()

append() method only works for the addition of elements at the end of the List, for the addition of elements at the desired position, insert() method is used. Unlike append() which takes only one argument, the insert() method requires two arguments(position, value).

Code:
```
#Just Search us on YouTube- "CONCEPT STUDY POINT"
emp=["Concept Classes",1001,"Jaipur","Rajasthan"]
emp.insert(2,"8 to 12")
```
Output:
['Concept Classes', 1001, '8 to 12', 'Jaipur','Rajasthan']

count()

The count() method returns the number of elements with the specified value. The count() function is used to count elements on a list as well as a string.

Code:
```
# Python list count() Method
# Creating a list
a = ['C','O','N','C','E','P','T']
# Method calling
c = a.count('C')
# Displaying result
print("count of C :",c)
```
Output:
count of C : 2

find()

Python find() method finds substring in the whole string and returns the index of the first match. It returns -1 if substring does not match.

```
a = ['C','O','N','C','E','P','T']
b="Our YouTube Channel is Concept Study Point"
c=b.find("Channel")
print("The Word Found on Position :", c)
print(b.find("f"))
    Output:
The Word Found on Position: 12
-1
```

remove()

Python List remove() is an inbuilt function in the Python programming language that removes a given object from the List.

```
    Code:
# Creating a list
a = ['C','O','N','C','E','P','T']
a.remove("O")
print(a)
    Output:
['C', 'N', 'C', 'E', 'P', 'T']
```

pop()

The python pop() method pops an element from the set. It does not take any argument but returns the popped element. It raises an error if the element is not present in the set.

```
    Code:
a=[1,2,3,4,5,6]
x=a.pop(1)
print(x)
print(a)
    Output
[1, 3, 4, 5, 6]
```

reverse()

The reverse() method reverses the sorting order of the elements. Python reverse() method reverses elements of the list. If the list is empty, it simply returns an empty list. After reversing the last index value of the list will be present at 0 index.

```
    Code :
a=[1,2,3,4,5,6]
x=a.pop(1)
print(a)
a.reverse()
print(a)
```

Output:
[1, 3, 4, 5, 6]
[6, 5, 4, 3, 1]

sort()

Python sort() method sorts the list elements. It also sorts the items into descending and ascending order. It takes an optional parameter 'reverse' which sorts the list into descending order. By default, list sorts the elements into ascending order.

Code:
```
a=[2,4,6,5,1,9]
x=a.pop(1)
print(a)
a.reverse()
print("The number after reverse",a)
a.sort()
print("The number after Sorting:", a)
```

Output:
[2, 6, 5, 1, 9]
The number after reverse [9, 1, 5, 6, 2]
The number after Sorting: [1, 2, 5, 6, 9]

min()

Python min() function is used to get the smallest element from the collection. This function takes two arguments, the first is a collection of elements and the second is key and returns the smallest element from the collection.

There are two types of min function –
1. min() functions with objects
2. min() functions with an iterable

1. min() functions with objects

Code:
```
a=['c','o','n','e','p','t']
b=[23,43,66,32,47,89]
print("the min alphabet value ", min(a))
print("the min number is ",min(b))
print("the max number is ",max(a))
```

Output:
the min alphabet value c
the min number is 23
the max number is t

2. min() functions with an iterable

When an iterable is passed to the min function it returns the smallest item of the iterable.

Code:
```
print("the max number from list is ",min([4, 12, 43.3, 19])) //list is used
d = {1: "c", 2: "b", 3: "a"} //using Dictionary
print("the min number in dictionary is ",min(d))
```

Output:
the max number from list is 4

the min number in dictionary is 1

the min number in dictionary is 1

FIVE

FLOW OF CONTROL & LOOPS

Python if else

Decision-making statements in programming languages decide the direction of the flow of program execution. In Python, if-else elif statement is used for decision making. As the name implies, decision-making allows us to run a particular block of code for a particular decision. Here, the decisions are made on the validity of the particular conditions. Condition checking is the backbone of decision-making.

If Statment :

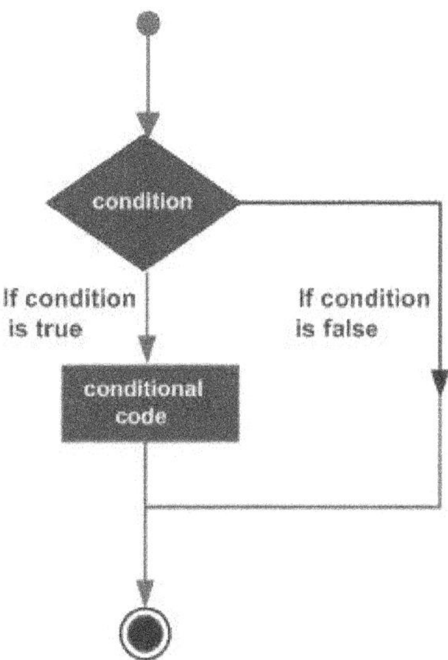

If Statment

The if statement is used to test a particular condition and if the condition is true, it executes a block of code known as if-block. The condition of if statement can be any valid logical expression that can be either evaluated to true or false.

Python supports the usual logical conditions from mathematics:

1. Equals: a == b
2. Not Equals: a != b
3. Less than: a < b
4. Less than or equal to: a <= b
5. Greater than: a > b
6. Greater than or equal to: a >= b

Syntax :
if condition:
 # Statements to execute if condition is true
  Code:
x=int(input("Enter a Value less than 10 : "))
if(x>10):
print("you enter a value greater than 10: ",x) // this statement print if & only if you enter a value >10
  Output:
Enter a Value less than 10 : 15
you enter a value greater than 10: 15
  Note : colon(:) is compulsory if we use "if" Control Statement

if-else statement

The if-else statement is similar to if statement except the fact that, it also provides the block of the code for the false case of the condition to be checked. If the condition provided in the if statement is false, then the else statement will be executed.
Syntax :
if condition:
  #block of statements
  else:
  #another block of statements (else-block)

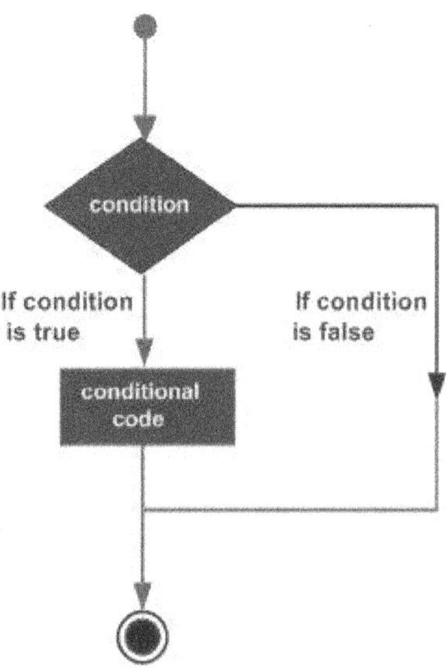

if-else Statement Block

  Code :

```
    age=int(input("Please Enter Your age :"))
if(age>18):
print("You are Eligible for Vote")
else :
print("You are Not Eligible for Vote")
    Output :
    Please Enter Your age :21
You are Eligible for Vote
```

Python nested loops

Python programming language allows to use one loop inside another loop.

```
    Code:
    a=int (input("Enter I Number: "))
b=int (input("Enter II Number: "))
c=int (input("Enter III Number: "))
if(a>b and a>c):
print("The I number is Greater : ",a)
elif(b>a and b>c):
print("The II Number is Greater : ",b)
else:
print("The III Number is Greater : ",c)
    Output:
Enter I Number: 15
Enter II Number: 17
Enter III Number: 6
The II Number is Greater: 17
```

While loops :

A while loop statement in Python programming language repeatedly executes a target statement as long as a given condition is true. The syntax of a while loop in Python is:

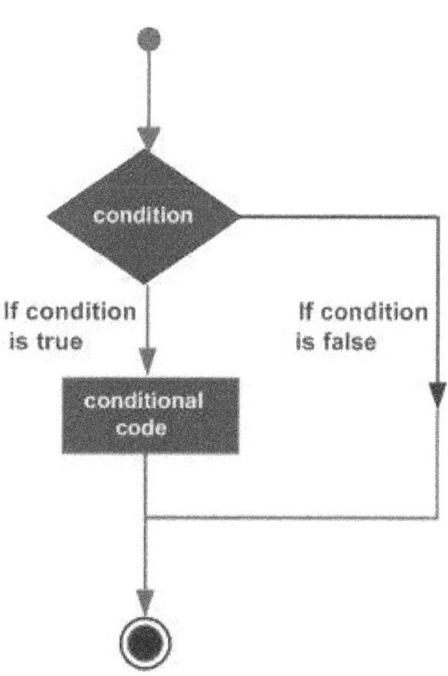

Loop Flow

While expression:
statement(s)

Code:

```
i=1
while i<=10 :
print(i)
i=i+1
```

Output:

```
1
2
3
4
5
6
7
8
9
10
```

Continue Statement :

When the continue statement is encountered, the control transfer to the beginning of the loop.

Code :

```
i=0
a="ConceptClasses"
while i<len(a):
print(i,'\t',a[i])
i=i+1
```

Output :

```
0 C
1 o
2 n
3 c
4 e
5 p
6 t
7 C
8 l
9 a
10 s
11 s
12 e
13 s
```

Break Statement :

The break statement is used to terminate the loop or statement in which it is present. After that, the control will pass to the statements that are present after the break statement, if available. If the break statement is present in the nested loop, then it terminates only those loops which contains break statement.

Code :

```
i=0
a="ConceptClasses"
while i<len(a):
print(i,'\t',a[i])
i=i+1
if a[i]!='n':
break
```

Output:

```
0 C
```

For Loop

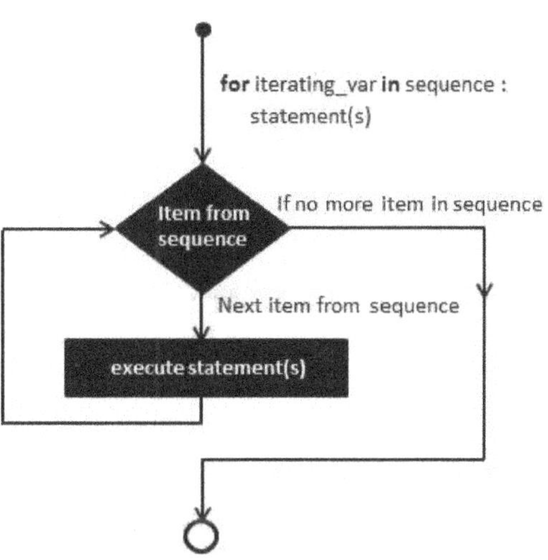

For Loop

For loops are used for sequential traversal. For example: traversing a list or string or array etc. The for loop is used in the case where we need to execute some part of the code until the given condition is satisfied. The for loop is also called a pre-tested loop. It is better to use for loop if the number of iterations is known in advance.

The for loop in Python is used to iterate over a sequence (such as a list, tuple, or string) or other iterable objects and execute a block of code for each item in the sequence. The general syntax of a for loop is as follows:

Code 1 :

```
for i in range(1, 6):
print(i)
```

Output:

```
1
2
3
4
```

5
Code 2 :
 # Start at 2, end at 10 (exclusive), step by 2
for i in range(2,16,2):
print(i)
youtube = ['Concept', 'Study', 'Point']
for study in youtube:
print(study)

Output:
2
4
6
8
10
12
14
Concept
Study
Point
Note that the variable **Study** takes on the value of each item in the list **youtube** on each iteration of the loop.

Nested Loop

Nested loops are a type of loop in Python where one loop is placed inside another loop. The inner loop is executed multiple times for each iteration of the outer loop. This is a useful technique when you need to perform a certain operation on each element of a nested data structure like a list of lists.

Coding :

```
num1 = [12, 13, 14]
num2 = [2, 3, 6]
for x in num1:
for y in num2:
print(x*y)
print(x*y)
```

Output :
24
36
72
26
39
78
28
42
84
84

SIX
STRING & ITS FUNCTIONS

What is String?

Single or double quotation marks surround strings in Python. 'hello' is the same as "hello".

Strings are a fundamental data type in Python used to store and manipulate text. Python string is the collection of characters surrounded by single quotes, double quotes, or triple quotes. The computer does not understand the characters; internally, it stores manipulated characters as a combination of the 0's and 1's.

Strings indexing and splitting: Like other languages, the indexing of the Python strings starts from 0. For example, The string "HELLO" is indexed as given in the below figure.

Code:

```
#Using single quotes
str1 = 'Concept'
print(str1)
#Using double quotes
str2 = "Study Point"
print(str2)
#Using triple quotes
str3 = '''Triple quotes are generally used for
represent the multiline or
docstring'''
print(str3)
```

Output:

```
Concept
Study Point
Triple quotes are generally used for
represent the multiline or
docstring
```

String Operators

Python provides a number of operators that can be used to manipulate strings. Here are some of the most commonly used ones:

1. Concatenation (+): This operator joins two or more strings together. For example, "hello " + "world" will result in "hello world".

2. Repetition (*): This operator is used to repeat a string a given number of times. For example, "hello " * 3 will result in "hello hello hello ".

3. Membership (in, not in): These operators are used to check if a string is present in another string. For example, "l" in "hello" will return True, while "z" in "hello" will return False.

4. Indexing ([]): This operator is used to access a specific character in a string. For example, "hello"[0] will return "h".

5. Slicing ([start:end]): This operator is used to extract a portion of a string. For example, "hello"[1:4] will return "ell".

6. Length (len()): This function is used to get the length of a string. For example, len("hello") will return 5.

It's important to note that strings in Python are immutable, meaning that you can't change the characters in a string once it has been created. However, you can create a new string by concatenating or slicing existing strings.

Code:

1. Concatenation (+)
first_name = "Concept"
last_name = "Classes"
full_name = first_name + " " + last_name
print(full_name)
> **Output: "Concept Classes"**
> **2. Repetition (*)**
greeting = "Python, "
print(greeting * 3)
> **Output: "Python, Python, Python, "**
> **3. Membership (in, not in)**
sentence = "The quick brown fox jumps over the lazy dog"
print("fox" **in** sentence) # Output: True
print("cat" **not in** sentence) # Output: True
print("cat" **in** sentence) # Output: False
> **4. Indexing ([])**
word = "Python"
print(word[0]) # Output: "P"
print(word[-1]) # Output: "n"
> **5. Slicing ([start:end])**
sentence = "The quick brown fox jumps over the lazy dog"
print(sentence[4:9])
print(sentence[:3])
print(sentence[20:])
> # Output: "quick"
Output: "The"
Output: "jumps over the lazy dog"
> **6. Length (len())**
word = "Python"
print(len(word)) #Output: 6

String Traversing In Python

In Python, while operating with String, one can do multiple operations on it. Let's see how to iterate over the characters of a string in Python. Traversing a string in Python, means iterating over each character or element of the string in order to access, process, or manipulate them individually. Traversing a string allows you to examine or modify the contents of the string, perform string manipulation operations, or extract information from the string based on specific conditions. Traversing a string can be done using various techniques, including using a for loop, indexing, or built-in string methods. The purpose of traversing a string is to work with each character in the string, either individually or collectively, to perform desired tasks or operations.

1. Iterating over characters using a for loop:

Code:

```
my_string = "Concept, Classes!"
for character in my_string :
print(character)
```

Output:

```
C
o
n
c
e
p
t
,

C
l
a
s
s
e
s
!
```

2. Accessing individual characters using indexing:

You can access individual characters in a string using square brackets ([]) and the index of the character. Indexing in Python starts from 0 for the first character, -1 for the last character, and so on.

Code

```
my_string = "Concept Study Point"
print(my_string[0]) # Output: C
print(my_string[6]) # Output: t
print(my_string[-1]) # Output: t
```

capitalize() method:

The capitalize() method converts the first character of a string to uppercase and makes all other characters lowercase.

Code:

```
my_string = "concept Study Point!"
capitalized_string = my_string.capitalize()
print(capitalized_string)
```

Output:

```
Concept study point!
```

title() method:

The title() method converts the first character of each word in a string to uppercase and makes all other characters lowercase. It capitalizes the first character of each word, based on whitespace or punctuation as separators.

Code :

```
my_string = "concept classes"
capitalized_string = my_string.title()
print(capitalized_string)
```

Output:

Concept Classes

In Python, strings provide several useful functions for manipulating and analyzing text. Here are three commonly used functions for string manipulation: lower(), upper(), and count().

lower() Method:

In Python, the lower() method is a string method that converts all the characters in a string to lowercase. It returns a new string with the lowercase representation of the original string.

Code:

```
my_string = "SUBSCRIBE OUR YOUTUBE CHANNEL"
lower_string = my_string.lower()
print(lower_string)
```

Output:

subscribe our youtube channel

Upper() Method:

upper(): The upper() method converts all characters in a string to uppercase. It returns a new string with the uppercase representation of the original string.

Code:

```
string = "Concept Study Point"
uppercase_string = string.upper()
print(uppercase_string)
```

Output:

CONCEPT STUDY POINT

find(substring) Method:

The find() method searches for a specified substring within a string and returns the index of the first occurrence. If the substring is not found, it returns -1.

Code:

```
string = "Hello how are you?"
index = string.find("are")
print(index)
index = string.find("Concept")
print(index)
```

Output :

```
10
-1
```

endswith(suffix):

The endswith() method checks whether a string ends with a specified suffix. It returns True if the string ends with the suffix, and False otherwise.

Code:

```
string = "Hello, How are You !"
a = string.endswith("world!")
print(a)
```

Output:

```
False
```

startswith(prefix):

The startswith() method checks whether a string starts with a specified prefix. It returns True if the string starts with the prefix, and False otherwise.

Code:

```
string = "Hello, world!"
a = string.startswith("Hello")
print(a)
```

Output:

```
True
```

isalnum() :

This function returns True if all the characters in the string are alphanumeric (letters or numbers), and False otherwise. It does not consider spaces or special characters.

Code:

```
text = "abc123"
print(text.isalnum()) # Output : True
    text = "abc123@"
print(text.isalnum()) # Output : False
```

isalpha() :

This function returns True if all the characters in the string are alphabetic (letters), and False otherwise. It does not consider spaces, numbers, or special characters.

Code:

```
text = "abc"
print(text.isalpha()) # Output : True
    text = "abc123"
print(text.isalpha()) # Output : False
```

isdigit() :

This function returns True if all the characters in the string are digits, and False otherwise. It does not consider spaces, letters, or special characters.

Code:

```
text = "123"
```

```
print(text.isdigit()) #Output : True
    text = "abc123"
print(text.isdigit()) # Output : False
```

islower() :

his function returns True if all the alphabetic characters in the string are lowercase, and False otherwise. It does not consider spaces, digits, or special characters.

```
    Code:
text = "abc"
print(text.islower()) # Output :True
    text = "Abc"
print(text.islower()) # Output :False
```

isupper() :

This function returns True if all the alphabetic characters in the string are uppercase, and False otherwise. It does not consider spaces, digits, or special characters.

```
    Code:
text = "ABC"
print(text.isupper()) # Output : True
    text = "Abc"
print(text.isupper()) #Output : False
```

isspace() :

This function returns True if all the characters in the string are whitespace characters (spaces, tabs, newlines, etc.), and False otherwise. It does not consider letters, digits, or special characters.

```
    Code:
text = " "
print(text.isspace()) # Output : True
    text = "Hello, world!"
print(text.isspace()) #Output : False
```

strip() :

This function is used to remove leading and trailing whitespace characters from a string. It returns a new string with the whitespace removed.

```
    Code:
text = " Hello, world! "
stripped_text = text.strip()
print(stripped_text)
    Output :
"Hello, world!"
```

Note: The original string text is not modified by the strip() function. It returns a new string with the desired changes.

lstrip(), rstrip(), replace(), join(), partition(), and split() Methods :

In Python, the string methods lstrip(), rstrip(), replace(), join(), partition(), and split() are used for various string manipulations.

1. strip(): This method removes leading and trailing whitespace characters (spaces, tabs, newlines) from a string and returns the modified string.

2. lstrip(): Similar to strip(), but it only removes leading whitespace characters from a string.

3. rstrip(): Similar to strip(), but it only removes trailing whitespace characters from a string.

4. replace(old, new): This method replaces all occurrences of the substring old with the substring new within a string. It returns a new string with the replacements.

5. join(iterable): This method concatenates the elements of an iterable (such as a list or tuple) into a single string, with each element separated by the string on which the method was called.

6. partition(separator): This method splits a string into three parts based on the first occurrence of a separator. It returns a tuple containing the part before the separator, the separator itself, and the part after the separator.

7. split(separator): This method splits a string into a list of substrings based on a separator. By default, the separator is whitespace. It returns a list of substrings.

Code:

```python
# strip(), lstrip(), rstrip(), replace(), join(), partition(), and split()
    # replace()
text = "Hello, World!"
new_text = text.replace("Hello", "Hi")
print(new_text) # Output: "Hi, World!"
    # join()
words = ["Hello", "World!"]
joined_text = ", ".join(words)
print(joined_text) # Output: "Hello, World!"
    # partition()
text = "Concept, Study , Point, Jaipur"
part1, sep, part2 = text.partition("Study")
print(part1) # Output: "Concept"
print(sep) # Output: "Study"
print(part2) # Output: ", Point, Jaipur"
    # split()
text = "apple,banana,orange"
fruits = text.split(",")
print(fruits) # Output: ['apple', 'banana', 'orange']
```

ᚦᚦᚦ

SEVEN

LIST

In Python, a list is a built-in data structure that represents an ordered collection of elements. It is one of the most commonly used data structures in Python due to its flexibility and versatility. Lists are mutable, which means their elements can be modified after they are created.

Lists in Python are defined by enclosing a comma-separated sequence of elements within square brackets ([]).

Lists can contain elements of different data types, including integers, floats, strings, or even other lists. For instance:

mixed_list = [1, 2.5, "Hello", [4, 5, 6]]

Lists also support indexing and slicing. Each element in a list has an index, starting from 0 for the first element. You can access individual elements by specifying their index within square brackets ([]). Lists can be modified by assigning new values to specific indices.

my_list = [1, 2, 3, 4, 5]
print(my_list[0]) # Output: 1
print(my_list[2]) # Output: 3

Lists are versatile and can be used in various programming scenarios to store, manipulate, and process collections of data efficiently.

LIST Operations :

1. Concatenation:

Concatenation is the process of combining two or more lists into a single list. In Python, you can use the + operator to concatenate lists.

2. Repetition :

Repetition allows you to create a new list by repeating the elements of an existing list. You can use the * operator to repeat a list.

3. Membership :

Membership allows you to check if an element is present in a list. You can use the 'in' operator to check for membership.

4. Slicing :

Slicing allows you to extract a portion of a list by specifying a range of indices. You can use the ':' operator for slicing.

These operations provide flexibility when working with lists in Python, allowing you to manipulate and extract data efficiently.

Code:

```
list1 = ['c','o','n']
list2 = ['c','e','p','t']
combined_list = list1 + list2
print(combined_list)
my_list = [1, 2, 3]
repeated_list = my_list * 3
print(repeated_list)
my_list = [1, 2, 3, 4, 5]
print(3 in my_list) # Check if 3 is present in the list
print(6 in my_list) # Check if 6 is present in the list
my_list = [1, 2, 3, 4, 5]
sliced_list = my_list[1:4] # Extract elements from index 1 to 3 (exclusive)
print(sliced_list)
```

Output:

```
['c', 'o', 'n', 'c', 'e', 'p', 't']
[1, 2, 3, 1, 2, 3, 1, 2, 3]
True
False
[2, 3, 4]
```

Traversing a LIST in Python

To traverse or iterate over a list in Python, you can use various methods, including loops and list comprehension. Here are a few common ways to traverse a list in Python:

1. **Using a for loop :**

Code:

```
my_list = [1, 2, 3, 4, 5]
for item in my_list:
print(item)
```

Output:

```
1
2
3
4
5
```

2. **Using a while loop with an index :**

```
my_list = [1, 2, 3, 4, 5]
index = 0
while index < len(my_list):
print(my_list[index])
index += 1
```

Output:

```
1
2
```

```
3
4
5
```

3. Using list comprehension :

Code :
```
my_list = [1, 2, 3, 4, 5]
    [print(item) for item in my_list]
```

Built-in function in List :

1. **len( ) :** The len() function in Python is used to determine the number of elements or items in an object. When applied to a list, len() returns the number of elements present in that list.

   Code:
   ```
   my_list = [1, 2, 3, 4, 5]
   length = len(my_list)
   print(length)
   ```

   Output :
   ```
   5
   ```

2. **list( ):** The list() function in Python is used to create a new list object. When called with an iterable as an argument, such as a string, tuple, or another list, it converts the iterable into a new list.

   Code:
   ```
   my_string = "Concept"
   my_list = list(my_string)
   print(my_list)
   ```

   Output :
   ```
   ['C', 'o', 'n', 'c', 'e', 'p', 't']
   ```
   In this example, the list() function is used to convert the string **"Concept"** into a list. Each character in the string becomes an individual element in the resulting list.

3. **append( ):** The append() method in Python is used to add an element to the end of a list. It modifies the original list by adding the specified item as a new element.

   Code :
   ```
   my_list = [1, 2, 3]
   my_list.append(4)
   print(my_list)
   ```

   Output :
   ```
   [1, 2, 3, 4]
   ```
   You can also append other data types or even other lists.

   Code :
   ```
   my_list = [1, 2, 3]
   my_list.append("Concept")
   my_list.append([5, 6, 7])
   print(my_list)
   ```

   Output:

[1, 2, 3, 'Concept', [5, 6, 7]]

4. **extend( ):** The extend() method in Python is used to append multiple elements from an iterable to the end of a list. It modifies the original list by adding the elements of the specified iterable.

Code:
```
my_list = [1, 2, 3]
my_list.extend("Hello")
my_list.extend((4, 5, 6))
my_list.extend([7, 8, 9])
print(my_list)
```

Output:
[1, 2, 3, 'H', 'e', 'l', 'l', 'o', 4, 5, 6, 7, 8, 9]

In this example, the extend() method is used to add elements from different iterables: the string "Hello", the tuple (4, 5, 6), and the list [7, 8, 9]. The modified list is then printed, resulting in [1, 2, 3, 'H', 'e', 'l', 'l', 'o', 4, 5, 6, 7, 8, 9] being displayed.

5. **insert()** : The insert() method in Python is used to insert an element at a specified index position within a list. It modifies the original list by shifting existing elements to accommodate the new element.

Code:
```
my_list = [1, 2, 3, 4]
my_list.insert(2, 5)
print(my_list)
```

Output :
[1, 2, 5, 3, 4]

In this example, the insert() method is called on the my_list list and passed two arguments: the index 2 and the element 5. The insert() method inserts the element 5 at index 2, shifting the existing elements after that index. Afterward, the modified list is printed, resulting in [1, 2, 5, 3, 4] being displayed.

6. **count( )** : The count() method in Python is used to count the number of occurrences of a specific element within a list. It returns the count as an integer value.

Code:
```
my_list = [1, 2, 2, 3, 4, 2, 5]
count = my_list.count(2)
print(count)
```

Output :
3

7. **index( )** : The index() method in Python is used to find the index of the first occurrence of a specified element within a list. It returns the index as an integer value.

Code:
```
my_list = [1, 2, 3, 4, 2, 5]
index = my_list.index(2, 2, 5)
print(index)
index = my_list.index(2, 2, 5)
print(index)
```

Output :
1
4

In this example, the index() method is called with the argument 2, and the start and end parameters are provided as 2 and 5 respectively. The index() method searches for 2 starting from index 2 (inclusive) up to index 5 (exclusive). It finds the second occurrence of 2 at index 4 within that range and returns it. The index is then printed, resulting in 4 being displayed.

8. **remove( ):** Removing elements from a list, To remove a specific element from a list, you can use the remove() method.

9. **reverse( ):** Reversing a list, To reverse the order of elements in a list, you can use the reverse() method. Example: my_list.reverse()

10. **sort( ):** Sorting a list, To sort a list in ascending order, you can use the sort() method. Example: my_list.sort()

11. **sorted( ):** Getting a sorted version of a list without modifying the original list. To get a new sorted list without modifying the original list, you can use the sorted() function. Example: sorted_list = sorted(my_list)

Code with Output :

```python
my_list = [5, 3, 8, 1, 2]
# Removing an element
my_list.remove(3)
print(my_list) # Output: [5, 8, 1, 2]
# Reversing the list
my_list.reverse()
print(my_list) # Output: [2, 1, 8, 5]
# Sorting the list
my_list.sort()
print(my_list) # Output: [1, 2, 5, 8]
# Getting a sorted version without modifying the original list
sorted_list = sorted(my_list)
print(sorted_list) # Output: [1, 2, 5, 8]
print(my_list) # Output: [1, 2, 5, 8] (original list remains unchanged)
```

12. **pop():** In Python, the pop() method is used to remove and return an element from a list based on its index.

Code:

```python
my_list = [1, 2, 3, 4, 5]
# Remove and return the element at index 2
removed_element = my_list.pop(2)
print("Removed element:", removed_element)
print("Updated list:", my_list)
```

Output :

```
Removed element: 3
Updated list: [1, 2, 4, 5]
```

13. **min( )**
14. **max( )**
15. **sum( )**

To find the minimum, maximum, and sum of a list in Python, you can use built-in functions and methods.

Code :

```python
my_list = [5, 2, 9, 1, 7]
minimum = min(my_list)
maximum = max(my_list)
total_sum = sum(my_list)
```

```
    print("Minimum:", minimum)
print("Maximum:", maximum)
print("Sum:", total_sum)
    Output :
Minimum: 1
Maximum: 9
Sum: 24
```

⊳⊳⊳

EIGHT

TUPLES

In Python, a tuple is an ordered collection of elements, which can be of different data types. Tuples are similar to lists, but unlike lists, tuples are immutable, meaning their elements cannot be modified once created.

Tuples also support negative indexing, where -1 refers to the last element, -2 refers to the second-to-last element, and so on.

Tuples can be used in various scenarios, such as returning multiple values from a function, representing coordinates or points in a multidimensional space, or as keys in dictionaries when immutability is required.

Since tuples are immutable, you cannot modify their elements or add/remove elements once they are created. However, you can perform operations like concatenation and slicing on tuples to create new tuples.

Definition: A tuple is an ordered collection of elements, enclosed in parentheses (), where the elements are separated by commas. Tuples are similar to lists, but they are immutable, meaning their elements cannot be changed after creation.

Immutable Nature: The immutability of tuples means that you cannot modify, add, or remove individual elements. However, you can perform operations on tuples to create new tuples.

Heterogeneous Elements: Tuples can contain elements of different data types, such as integers, floats, strings, booleans, or even other tuples. For example my_tuple = (1, 2.5, 'Hello', True)

Concatenation, Repetition, Membership, and Slicing

Concatenation, repetition, membership, and slicing are all operations commonly used with strings or sequences in programming languages.

1. **Concatenation:** Concatenation is the process of combining two or more strings or sequences into a single string or sequence. In programming, you can concatenate strings using the concatenation operator, which is usually represented by the plus symbol (+). For example, if you have two strings "Hello" and "world", concatenating them would result in the string "Hello world".

2. **Repetition:** Repetition, also known as replication or duplication, involves repeating a string or sequence a certain number of times. This operation is useful when you need to create a longer string by repeating a smaller string multiple times. In most programming languages, you can repeat a string using the multiplication operator (*). For example, if you repeat the string "abc" three times, you would get "abcabcabc".

3. **Membership:** Membership refers to checking whether an element or substring exists within a string or sequence. It allows you to determine if a particular value is present in a given sequence. In many programming languages, you can use the membership operator (such as "in" or "not in") to perform this check. For instance, you can check if the substring "world" is present in the string "Hello world" by using the expression "world" in "Hello world", which would evaluate to true.

4. **Slicing:** Slicing involves extracting a portion (or a slice) of a string or sequence based on a specified range or index. It allows you to extract substrings or subsequences from a larger sequence. Typically, you specify the starting and ending indices of the slice to indicate the range you want to extract. The resulting slice includes all elements from

the starting index up to, but not including, the ending index. Slicing is commonly represented using square brackets ([]). For example, if you have the string "Hello world", you can slice it to get "Hello" by using the expression "Hello world"[0:5].

Code:

```
tuple1 = (1, 2, 3)
tuple2 = (4, 5, 6)
concatenated_tuple = tuple1 + tuple2
print(concatenated_tuple) # Output: (1, 2, 3, 4, 5, 6)
    repeated_tuple = tuple1 * 3
print(repeated_tuple)
    print(2 in tuple1) #Membership: You can check if an element is present in a tuple using the in operator.
print(4 in tuple1)
    tuple1 = (1, 2, 3, 4, 5, 6)
sliced_tuple = tuple1[1:4] # Elements from index 1 to 3 (exclusive)
print(sliced_tuple) # Output: (2, 3, 4)
    # You can also specify a step size:
step_tuple = tuple1[::2] # Every second element
print(step_tuple) # Output: (1, 3, 5)
```

Output :

```
(1, 2, 3, 4, 5, 6)
(1, 2, 3, 1, 2, 3, 1, 2, 3)
True
False
(2, 3, 4)
(1, 3, 5)
```

Built-In Functions:

In Python, tuples are an immutable sequence type, and they come with several built-in functions that can be used to perform various operations.

1. **len()** - Returns the number of elements in a tuple.
2. **min()** - Returns the smallest element in a tuple.
3. **max()** - Returns the largest element in a tuple.
4. **sum()** - Returns the sum of all elements in a tuple (works if the elements are numeric).
5. **tuple()** - Converts an iterable (list, string, etc.) into a tuple.
6. **sorted()** - Returns a new sorted list from the elements of a tuple.
7. **count()** - Returns the number of occurrences of a specific element in a tuple.

Code:

```
    my_tuple = (2, 10, 8, 4, 5,2,2)
print("Length is : ",len(my_tuple),"\n") # Output: 5
    print("Min Value is : ", min(my_tuple),"\n")
    print("Max Value is : ",max(my_tuple),"\n")
    print("the Sum of Tuple is : ",sum(my_tuple),"\n")
    my_list = [1, 2, 3, 4, 5]
converted_tuple = tuple(my_list)
print("Convert list into tuple :",converted_tuple,"\n")
```

```
    sorted_list = sorted(my_tuple)
print("Sorted tuple is :", sorted_list,"\n")
    print("Count value in Tuple: ", my_tuple.count(2),"\n")
    print("Index Tuple : ", my_tuple.index(2)
```

OutPut:
Length is : 7
    Min Value is : 2
    Max Value is : 10
    the Sum of Tuple is : 33
    Convert list into tuple : (1, 2, 3, 4, 5)
    Sorted tuple is : [2, 2, 2, 4, 5, 8, 10]
    Count Tuple: 3
    Index Tuple : 0

8. **index()** - Returns the index of the first occurrence of a specific element in a tuple. The index() method is used to find the index of the first occurrence of a specific element in a tuple. It returns the index value if the element is found, otherwise, it raises a ValueError exception.

tuple_name.index(element, start, end)
tuple_name: The name of the tuple in which you want to find the index of the element.
element: The element for which you want to find the index.
start (optional): The index at which the search starts (inclusive). If not provided, the search starts from the beginning of the tuple.
end (optional): The index at which the search ends (exclusive). If not provided, the search continues until the end of the tuple.

Code:
```
    my_tuple = (10, 20, 30, 20, 40, 50)
    index_1 = my_tuple.index(20)
print(index_1) # Output: 1
    index_2 = my_tuple.index(20, 2)
print(index_2) # Output: 3
    index_3 = my_tuple.index(20, 2, 4)
print(index_3) # Output: 3
    index_4 = my_tuple.index(60) # Raises ValueError: tuple.index(x): x not in tuple
```

In the above example, index_1 returns the index of the first occurrence of 20 in the tuple. index_2 demonstrates searching for 20 starting from index 2. Similarly, index_3 restricts the search between indices 2 and 4. Finally, index_4 raises a ValueError because 60 is not present in the tuple.

Tuple Assignment :

Tuple assignment is a feature in many programming languages, including Python, that allows you to assign multiple variables at once using a single statement. It is particularly useful when you have a tuple or a sequence of values and you want to assign each value to a separate variable.

In Python, tuple assignment is done by placing the variables on the left-hand side and the values on the right-hand side, separated by the assignment operator (=). The number of variables on the left-hand side must match the number of values on the right-hand side.

```
    x, y = 10, 20
print(x) # Output: 10
```

print(y) # Output: 20

In this example, the values 10 and 20 are assigned to variables x and y, respectively, in a single statement. The first value is assigned to the first variable, and the second value is assigned to the second variable.

x = 10

y = 20

x, y = y, x

print(x) # Output: 20

print(y) # Output: 10

In this case, the values of x and y are swapped by assigning y to x and x to y in a single statement.

Tuple assignment can be used with tuples, lists, or any iterable object that contains the same number of elements as the number of variables on the left-hand side.

Nested Tuple :

In Python, you can create nested tuples, which are tuples that contain other tuples as elements. This allows you to represent and work with hierarchical or structured data.

Code:

nested_tuple = ((1, 2, 3), ('a', 'b', 'c'), (True, False))

print(nested_tuple[0]) # Output: (1, 2, 3)

print(nested_tuple[1][2]) # Output: 'c'

print(nested_tuple[2][1]) # Output: False

In the above code, nested_tuple[0] accesses the first element of nested_tuple, which itself is a tuple (1, 2, 3). nested_tuple[1][2] accesses the third element of the second element of nested_tuple, which is the value 'c'. Similarly, nested_tuple[2][1] accesses the second element of the third element of nested_tuple, which is the value False.

Code:

a, (b, c), d = (1, (2, 3), 4)

print(a) # Output: 1

print(b) # Output: 2

print(c) # Output: 3

print(d) # Output: 4

In this case, the values (1, (2, 3), 4) are assigned to variables a, (b, c), and d using tuple assignment. The value 1 is assigned to a, the value (2, 3) is assigned to (b, c), and the value 4 is assigned to d.

NINE

DICTIONARY

Dictionary in Python is an unordered collection of data values, used to store data values like a map, which, unlike other Data Types that hold only a single value as an element, Dictionary holds key:value pair.

Python Dictionary is used to store the data in a key-value pair format. The dictionary is the data type in Python, which can simulate the real-life data arrangement where some specific value exists for some particular key. It is a mutable data structure. The dictionary is defined into element Keys and values.

Keys must be a single element. Value can be any type such as list, tuple, integer, etc.

1. How to Create a Dictionary :

Code:

```
a=dict({1:"hi",2:"how are you",3:[123]})
print(a)
print(type(a)) //Type of Datatypes
print(a[2])
```

Output:

```
{1: 'hi', 2: 'how are you', 3: [123]}
<class 'dict'>
how are you
```

2. How to update a Dictionary :

The update() method will update the dictionary with the items from the given argument.

Code :

```
a=dict({1:"hi",2:"how are you",3:[123],"City":"Jaipur",4:""})
print(a)
#print(a[2])
a[2]="I am From Concept Classes"
print(a)
a.update({"City":"Delhi"})
print(a)
```

Output:

```
{1: 'hi', 2: 'how are you', 3: [123], 'City': 'Jaipur', 4: ''}
{1: 'hi', 2: 'I am From Concept Classes', 3: [123], 'City': 'Jaipur', 4: ''} //Update Dictionary
{1: 'hi', 2: 'I am From Concept Classes', 3: [123], 'City': 'Delhi', 4: ''} //Update Dictionary
```

3. How to Delete data from a Dictionary :

The items of the dictionary can be deleted by using the **del** keyword.

Code:

```
a=dict({1:"hi",2:"how are you",3:[123],"City":"Jaipur",4:""})
print(a)
del a[3]
```

```
print("Dictionary After Delete Data : ",a)
    Output:
{1: 'hi', 2: 'how are you', 3: [123], 'City': 'Jaipur', 4: ''}
{1: 'hi', 2: 'how are you', 3: [123], 'City': 'Tonk', 4: ''}
Dictionary After Delete Data : {1: 'hi', 2: 'how are you', 'City': 'Tonk', 4: ''}
    4. How to input data in Dictionary :
    Code:
a=dict({1:"hi",2:"how are you",3:[123],"City":"Jaipur",4:""})
print(a)
a[1]=input("Enter Name: ")
a[4]=input("Enter Address: ")
print("Dictionary After Input Data : ",a)
    Output :
{1: 'hi', 2: 'how are you', 3: [123], 'City': 'Jaipur', 4: ''}
Enter Name: Hello
Enter Address: Delhi
Dictionary After Input Data : {1: 'Hello', 2: 'how are you', 3: [123], 'City': 'Jaipur', 4: 'Delhi'}
```

Dictionary Methods & Built-in Functions

1. len()

Dictionaries in Python are a collection of key-value pairs of data. These are used in many manipulations in Python and are one of the most important data structures in python. To calculate the length of the dictionary, the built-in len() method is used. This in-built method takes a Python object as an argument and returns the number of items in it. It can be used on strings, lists, dictionaries, tuples, and sets.

```
    Code:
a=dict({1:"hi",2:"how are you",3:[123],"4:City":"Jaipur",5:""})
print(a)
print("the length of dictionary : ",len(a))
    Output:
{1: 'hi', 2: 'how are you', 3: [123], '4:City': 'Jaipur', 5: ''}
the length of dictionary : 5
```

2. dict()

Creates a dictionary from a sequence of key-value pairs.

```
    Code 5.
a=dict({1:"hi",2:"how are you",3:[123],"4:City":"Jaipur",5:""})
print(a)
print("the length of dictionary : ",len(a))
b=dict(a) //Dictionary 'b' is created
print(b)
    Output :
{1: 'hi', 2: 'how are you', 3: [123], '4:City': 'Jaipur', 5: ''}
```

the length of dictionary : 5
{1: 'hi', 2: 'how are you', 3: [123], '4:City': 'Jaipur', 5: ''}

3. del()

The del keyword is used to delete objects. In Python everything is an object, so the del keyword can also be used to delete variables, lists, parts of a list, etc.

Code:

```
con=dict({1:"Hello", 2:"How are You?" , 3:45689, 4:[123],5:""})
del con[2]
print("Second Value Deleted: ",con)
```

Output:

Second Value Deleted: {1: 'Hello', 3: 45689, 4: [123], 5: 'x'}

4. keys()

keys() method in Python Dictionary, returns a view object that displays a list of all the keys in the dictionary in order of insertion. Python keys() method is used to fetch all the keys from the dictionary. It returns a list of keys and an empty list if the dictionary is empty.

Code:

```
con=dict({1:"Hello",2:"How are You?",3:45689,4:[123],5:""})
x=con.keys()
print("The Keys of Con Dict is : ",x)
```

Output :

The Keys of Con Dict is : dict_keys([1, 2, 3, 4, 5])

5. items()

Python item() method returns a new view of the dictionary. This view is a collection of key-value tuples. This method does not take any parameter and returns an empty view if the dictionary is empty. items() method is used to return the list with all dictionary keys with values.

Code:

```
con=dict({1:"Hello",2:"How are You?",3:45689,4:[123],5:""})
x=con.items()
print("The Items of Con Dic",x)
```

Output:

The Items of Con Dic dict_items([(1, 'Hello'), (2, 'How are You?'), (3, 45689), (4, [123]), (5, 'aadil')])

6. values()

values() is an inbuilt method in the Python programming language that returns a view object. The view object contains the values of the dictionary, as a list. If you use the type() method on the return value, you get "dict_values object". It must be cast to obtain the actual list. The values() method returns a view object. The view object contains the values of the dictionary, as a list.

Code:

```
con=dict({1:"Hello",2:"How are You?",3:45689,4:[123],5:""})
x=con.values()
print("The Values of Con Dict is :",x)
```

Output :
The Values of Con Dict is : dict_values(['Hello', 'How are You?', 45689, [123], 'x'])

7. get()

The get() method returns the value of the item with the specified key. Python get() method return the value for the given key if present in the dictionary. If not, then it will return None (if get() is used with only one argument).
    Code:

```
con=dict({1:"Hello",2:"How are You?",3:45689,4:[123],5:""})
print("The 3 item is :",con.get(3))
```

    Output:
The 3 item is : 45689

8. clear()

The clear() method removes all items from the dictionary.
    Code:

```
con=dict({1:"Hello",2:"How are You?",3:45689,4:[123],5:""})
con.clear()
print("After Clear Function Use: ",con)
```

    Output :
After Clear Function Use: {}

9. update() :

This function is used to update a dictionary with the key-value pairs from another dictionary or an iterable object.

10. fromkeys() :

This function creates a new dictionary with the specified keys and a default value for all the keys.

11. copy() :

This function creates a shallow copy of a dictionary, returning a new dictionary with the same key-value pairs.

12. pop() :

This function removes and returns the value associated with a specified key from a dictionary. If the key is not found, it can optionally return a default value.

13. popitem() :

This function removes and returns an arbitrary key-value pair from a dictionary. It is useful when you want to remove and process items in an unordered manner.

14. setdefault() :

This function returns the value associated with a specified key in a dictionary. If the key is not found, it inserts the key with a default value and returns the default value.

15. max() :

This function returns the maximum value among the keys in a dictionary.

16. min() :

This function returns the minimum value among the keys in a dictionary.

17. count() :

This function is not a built-in function for dictionaries. It is used for counting occurrences of a specified element in a list or tuple.

18. sorted() :

This function returns a new sorted list of the keys in a dictionary.

Code :

```python
# Dictionary initialization
my_dict = {'apple': 5, 'banana': 3, 'orange': 7}
    # update()
new_dict = {'grape': 2, 'watermelon': 4}
my_dict.update(new_dict)
print(my_dict) # Output: {'apple': 5, 'banana': 3, 'orange': 7, 'grape': 2, 'watermelon': 4}
    # fromkeys()
keys = ['apple', 'banana', 'orange']
default_value = 0
new_dict = dict.fromkeys(keys, default_value)
print(new_dict) # Output: {'apple': 0, 'banana': 0, 'orange': 0}
    # copy()
copy_dict = my_dict.copy()
print(copy_dict) # Output: {'apple': 5, 'banana': 3, 'orange': 7, 'grape': 2, 'watermelon': 4}
    # pop()
value = my_dict.pop('apple')
print(value) # Output: 5
print(my_dict) # Output: {'banana': 3, 'orange': 7, 'grape': 2, 'watermelon': 4}
    # popitem()
key, value = my_dict.popitem()
print(key, value) # Output: 'watermelon' 4
print(my_dict) # Output: {'banana': 3, 'orange': 7, 'grape': 2}
    # setdefault()
default_value = my_dict.setdefault('apple', 0)
print(default_value) # Output: 0
print(my_dict) # Output: {'banana': 3, 'orange': 7, 'grape': 2, 'apple': 0}
```

```python
    # max()
max_key = max(my_dict)
print(max_key) # Output: 'orange'
    # min()
min_key = min(my_dict)
print(min_key) # Output: 'apple'
    # sorted()
sorted_keys = sorted(my_dict)
print(sorted_keys) # Output: ['apple', 'banana', 'grape', 'orange']
    # count() - Note that count() is not a built-in function for dictionaries.

    # max()
max_key = max(my_dict)
print(max_key) # Output: 'orange'
```

TEN

PYTHON MODULE

A Python module is a file containing Python code that defines functions, classes, and variables that can be reused in other programs. It provides a way to organize and package related code together for easy reuse and maintainability.

A module can contain any valid Python code, including function and class definitions, variable assignments, and executable statements. It is saved with a .py extension and can be imported into other Python programs using the import statement.

Here are some key points about Python modules:

1. Code Organization: Modules help in organizing code by separating it into logical units. Each module focuses on a specific functionality or set of related functionalities, making the code easier to understand and maintain.
2. Reusability: Modules facilitate code reuse. Once you have defined a module, you can import it into other programs and use its functions, classes, and variables without having to rewrite the code. This promotes code efficiency and reduces redundancy.
3. Namespace Isolation: Modules provide namespace isolation, meaning the names defined in a module do not conflict with names in other modules or the main program. This allows you to have variables or functions with the same name in different modules without causing conflicts.
4. Encapsulation: Modules encapsulate code by hiding internal implementation details. Only the functions, classes, and variables that you explicitly export (by using the from ... import statement) are accessible from outside the module. This helps in maintaining a clean and understandable interface.
5. Standard Library Modules: Python comes with a large standard library that includes numerous modules covering a wide range of functionalities. These modules are part of the Python distribution and are available for immediate use. Examples of standard library modules include math, os, datetime, random, and csv, among many others.

Third-Party Modules: In addition to the standard library, Python has a vast ecosystem of third-party modules and packages created by the Python community. These modules can be installed from external sources, such as the Python Package Index (PyPI), and provide additional functionality to extend the capabilities of Python.

By leveraging the power of modules, you can write modular, reusable, and maintainable code in Python. They allow you to break down complex tasks into smaller, manageable units and promote code organization and efficiency.

Python modules are reusable pieces of code that contain functions, classes, and variables. They help in organizing and reusing code by dividing it into logical units. Modules provide a way to package related code together and make it easily importable and accessible in other Python programs.

Python has a vast standard library that includes a wide range of modules covering various functionalities, such as file I/O, networking, mathematics, date and time operations, regular expressions, and more. These modules come bundled with the Python installation, so you can use them without any additional installations.

Importing Math Module :

To import the math module in Python, you can use the following code:

import math

This imports the entire math module, which provides various mathematical functions and constants for performing mathematical operations in Python. Once you've imported the math module, you can use its functions and constants in your code.

Code:

```
import math
x = 16
sqrt_x = math.sqrt(x)
print(sqrt_x)
```

Output:

```
4.0
```

In this example, we import the math module and use its sqrt() function to calculate the square root of the variable x, which is assigned the value 16. The result is then printed to the console.

Some Math Module/Functions in Python

1. Pi (π): The math.pi constant represents the mathematical constant pi, which is the ratio of a circle's circumference to its diameter. It is approximately equal to 3.14159.
2. Euler's number (e): The math.e constant represents Euler's number, which is a mathematical constant approximately equal to 2.71828. It is commonly used in exponential and logarithmic functions.
3. Square root (sqrt()): The math.sqrt() function returns the square root of a given number.
4. Ceiling (ceil()): The math.ceil() function returns the smallest integer greater than or equal to a given number.
5. Floor (floor()): The math.floor() function returns the largest integer less than or equal to a given number.
6. Power (pow()): The math.pow() function returns the value of a number raised to a specified power.
7. Absolute value (fabs()): The math.fabs() function returns the absolute (positive) value of a given number.

Code :

```
import math
    # Constants
print("Value of pi:", math.pi)
print("Value of e:", math.e)
    # Square root
print("Square root of 16:", math.sqrt(16))
    # Ceiling
print("Ceiling of 4.2:", math.ceil(4.2))
    # Floor
print("Floor of 4.2:", math.floor(4.2))
    # Power
print("2 raised to the power of 3:", math.pow(2, 3))
    # Absolute value
print("Absolute value of -4.5:", math.fabs(-4.5))
    Output:
    Value of pi: 3.141592653589793
Value of e: 2.718281828459045
Square root of 16: 4.0
```

Ceiling of 4.2: 5
Floor of 4.2: 4
2 raised to the power of 3: 8.0
Absolute value of -4.5: 4.5

8. Sin() :

In Python's math module, you can calculate the sine of an angle using the sin() function

Code:

```python
import math
    angle = 45 # Angle in degrees
radians = math.radians(angle) # Convert angle to radians
sin_value = math.sin(radians) # Calculate the sine
    print(sin_value)
```

Output:

0.7071067811865476

In the example above, the math.radians() function is used to convert the angle from degrees to radians because the sin() function in the math module expects the angle to be in radians. Then, the math.sin() function is called with the radians value to calculate the sine of the angle. The result is printed, which in this case is approximately 0.7071067811865476.

9. tan(): In Python's math module, you can calculate the tangent of an angle using the tan() function.

Code:

```python
import math
    angle = 30 # Angle in degrees
radians = math.radians(angle) # Convert angle to radians
tan_value = math.tan(radians) # Calculate the tangent
    print(tan_value)
```

Output: 0.5773502691896257

In the example above, the math.radians() function is used to convert the angle from degrees to radians because the tan() function in the math module expects the angle to be in radians. Then, the math.tan() function is called with the radians value to calculate the tangent of the angle. The result is printed, which in this case is approximately 0.5773502691896257.

10. Cos(): In Python's math module, you can calculate the cosine of an angle using the cos() function.

Code:

```python
import math
    angle = 60 # Angle in degrees
radians = math.radians(angle) # Convert angle to radians
cos_value = math.cos(radians) # Calculate the cosine
    print(cos_value)
```

Output: 0.5000000000000001

In the example above, the math.radians() function is used to convert the angle from degrees to radians because the cos() function in the math module expects the angle to be in radians. Then, the math.cos() function is called with the radians value to calculate the cosine of the angle. The result is printed, which in this case is approximately 0.5000000000000001.

Random Module in Python :

The random module in Python is a built-in module that provides functions for generating random numbers and making random selections. It is widely used in various applications such as games, simulations, statistical analysis, and cryptography.

The random module uses a pseudorandom number generator (PRNG) to generate random numbers. A PRNG is an algorithm that produces a sequence of numbers that appear to be random but are actually deterministic, meaning that given the same initial state or seed, it will produce the same sequence of numbers. The specific algorithm used by Python's random module is based on the Mersenne Twister, which is known for its long period and high-quality random numbers.

To use the random module, you need to import it into your Python script or interactive session using the import statement:

Code :

import random

Once imported, you can access various functions and methods provided by the module.

1. random():

   In Python, the random module is a built-in module that provides functions for generating random numbers. One of the functions in the random module is random(), which returns a random floating-point number between 0 and 1 (inclusive of 0 but exclusive of 1).

   Code:

   import random

   # Generate a random number between 0 and 1

   random_number = random.random()

   print(random_number)

   Output :

   0.123456789

   0.987654321

   0.456789123

2. randint():

   However, there is a similar function called randint() in the random module of Python's standard library. The randint() function generates a random integer between the specified range.

   Code:

   import random

   # Generate a random integer between 1 and 10

   random_number = random.randint(1, 10)

   print(random_number)

   Output:

   In this example, random.randint(1, 10) will generate a random integer between 1 and 10 (inclusive) and assign it to the variable random_number. The generated random number will be printed on the console.

3. randrange():

   The randrange() function is another function available in the random module of Python's standard library. It is used to generate a random integer from a specified range.

   The randrange() function has the following syntax:

random.randrange(start, stop[, step])
The start parameter specifies the start of the range (inclusive), while the stop parameter specifies the end of the range (exclusive). The optional step parameter can be used to specify the step size between values in the range.

Code:

```python
import random
    # Generate a random integer between 0 and 10 (exclusive of 10)
random_number = random.randrange(0, 10)
print(random_number)
```

Output:
In this example, random.randrange(0, 10) will generate a random integer between 0 and 10 (exclusive of 10) and assign it to the variable random_number. The generated random number will be printed on the console.

In Python, you can calculate the mean, median, and mode of a list of numbers using various libraries and functions. Here's an overview of how you can use some commonly used libraries and functions to calculate these statistical measures

4. The **statistics.mean()** function calculates the mean (average) of the data, **statistics.median()** function calculates the median, and **statistics.mode()** function calculates the mode.

Code:

```python
import statistics
data = [1, 2, 3, 4, 2, 5,7,8,9,2,3,5,6,7,3,5,66,7]
    # Mean
mean_value = statistics.mean(data)
print("Mean:", mean_value)
    # Median
median_value = statistics.median(data)
print("Median:", median_value)
    # Mode
mode_value = statistics.mode(data)
print("Mode:", mode_value)
    Output :
    Mean: 8.055555555555555
Median: 5.0
Mode: 2
```

ELEVEN
NUMPY

NumPy is a popular Python library that stands for "Numerical Python." It provides support for large, multi-dimensional arrays and matrices, along with a collection of mathematical functions to operate on these arrays efficiently. NumPy is widely used for scientific computing and data analysis tasks in Python.

Here are some key features and functionalities of NumPy:

Arrays: NumPy's main feature is the ndarray (n-dimensional array) object, which allows you to create and manipulate arrays of homogeneous data types efficiently. These arrays can have any number of dimensions and are much more efficient than Python lists for storing and manipulating large amounts of numerical data.

Mathematical Operations: NumPy provides various mathematical functions that operate element-wise on arrays. These include basic arithmetic operations (addition, subtraction, multiplication, division), trigonometric functions, exponential and logarithmic functions, statistical functions, and more. These functions can be applied to entire arrays or specific elements or axes.

Broadcasting: NumPy supports broadcasting, which is a powerful mechanism for performing arithmetic operations on arrays with different shapes. Broadcasting allows you to perform operations between arrays of different sizes and shapes by automatically extending the smaller array to match the shape of the larger array.

Array Manipulation: NumPy provides various functions for manipulating arrays, such as reshaping, transposing, concatenating, splitting, and indexing. These functions allow you to rearrange and extract data from arrays easily.

Efficient Computation: NumPy's operations are implemented in highly optimized C and Fortran code, making them much faster than equivalent Python loops. This efficiency is particularly beneficial when working with large datasets or performing complex numerical computations.

You can install NumPy using the following command:

pip install numpy

Once installed, you can import NumPy in your Python code using:

import numpy as np

NumPy Array:

A NumPy array, or ndarray, is a fundamental data structure provided by the NumPy library. It is a multidimensional, homogeneous array that stores elements of the same data type. The array can have one or more dimensions, and each dimension is called an "axis."

Some important characteristics of NumPy arrays include:

Homogeneous data type: All elements in a NumPy array must have the same data type. This allows for efficient storage and computation on arrays.

Fixed-size: NumPy arrays have a fixed size defined at the time of creation. Once created, the size of the array cannot be changed. However, you can create a new array with a different size and copy the data from the original array if needed.

N-dimensional: NumPy arrays can have any number of dimensions, allowing for the representation of complex data structures. For example, a 1-dimensional array represents a vector, a 2-dimensional array represents a matrix, and a 3-dimensional array represents a cube of data.

Efficient computation: NumPy arrays are designed for efficient numerical computations. They provide fast element-wise operations and vectorized functions, which means you can perform operations on entire arrays without writing explicit loops.

Creating a NumPy array is straightforward. Here's an example of creating a 1-dimensional array:

Code:

```python
import numpy as np
# Create a 1-dimensional array
arr = np.array([1, 2, 3, 4, 5])
print(arr)
```

Output:

```
[1 2 3 4 5]
```

NumPy arrays are widely used in scientific computing, data analysis, machine learning, and other fields due to their efficiency, versatility, and integration with other libraries in the Python ecosystem.

Creating a 2-D Array in numpy :

To create a 2-dimensional array, also known as a matrix, using NumPy, you can pass a nested list or a tuple of lists to the np.array() function. Each inner list represents a row in the matrix.

Code:

```python
import numpy as np
# Create a 2-D array
matrix = np.array([[1, 2, 3],
[4, 5, 6],
[7, 8, 9]])
print(matrix)
```

Output:

```
[[1 2 3]
[4 5 6]
[7 8 9]]
```

In this example, we created a 3x3 matrix with integer values. The outer list contains three inner lists, representing three rows. Each inner list holds the elements of the corresponding row.

Attributes of NumPy Array:

NumPy arrays, or ndarray objects, have several useful attributes that provide information about the array's shape, data type, memory layout, and more. Here are some commonly used attributes of NumPy arrays:

1. **shape:** This attribute returns a tuple representing the dimensions of the array. For a 2-D array, it indicates the number of rows and columns.

    Code:

    ```python
    import numpy as np
    arr = np.array([[1, 2, 3], [4, 5, 6]])
    print(arr.shape)

    # Output: (2, 3)
    ```

2. **dtype:** The dtype attribute specifies the data type of the elements in the array, such as int, float, bool, etc.
   Code:
```
import numpy as np
    arr = np.array([1, 2, 3], dtype=np.float64)
print(arr.dtype)
```

   #Output: float64
3. **size:** The size attribute returns the total number of elements in the array.
   Code:
```
import numpy as np
    arr = np.array([[1, 2, 3], [4, 5, 6]])
print(arr.size)
```

   #Output: 6
4. **ndim:** This attribute provides the number of dimensions (or axes) of the array.
   Code:
```
import numpy as np
    arr = np.array([[1, 2, 3], [4, 5, 6]])
print(arr.ndim)
```

   #Output: 2
5. **itemsize:** The itemsize attribute returns the size in bytes of each element in the array.
   Code:
```
import numpy as np
    arr = np.array([1, 2, 3], dtype=np.float64)
print(arr.itemsize)
```

   #Output: 8 (for float64, as each element takes 8 bytes)

Indexing & Slicing :

In NumPy, indexing refers to the process of accessing and manipulating elements of arrays or matrices using their position or indices. NumPy provides powerful indexing capabilities that go beyond what is available in standard Python lists.

NumPy supports several types of indexing techniques, including basic indexing, advanced indexing, and boolean indexing.

1. Basic indexing: NumPy arrays can be indexed using integers or slices. You can use integers to access specific elements at particular positions or use slices to extract a portion of the array. For example:

   Code:
```
import numpy as np
    arr = np.array([1, 2, 3, 4, 5])
print(arr[0]) # Output: 1
print(arr[2:4])
```

#Output: [3, 4]

2. Advanced indexing: NumPy allows indexing arrays with arrays of indices or arrays of boolean values. Advanced indexing creates a new array that is a copy of the original array. Here's an example:

Code:
```python
import numpy as np
    arr = np.array([1, 2, 3, 4, 5])
indices = np.array([0, 2, 4])
print(arr[indices])
```

#Output: [1, 3, 5]

3. Boolean indexing: You can use boolean expressions to index arrays. This method is particularly useful when you want to select elements based on certain conditions. Here's an example:

Code:
```python
import numpy as np
    arr = np.array([1, 2, 3, 4, 5])
condition = arr > 3
print(arr[condition])
```

#Output: [4, 5]

Slicing:

In NumPy, slicing refers to the process of extracting a portion of an array by specifying a range of indices. It allows you to extract a subarray from an existing array. Slicing in NumPy is similar to slicing in Python lists but provides more advanced capabilities.

The basic syntax for slicing in NumPy is as follows:

array[start:stop:step]

Here's a breakdown of each component:

start: The index where the slice starts (inclusive).

stop: The index where the slice ends (exclusive).

step (optional): The step size or the number of elements to skip between indices.

Code:
```python
import numpy as np
    arr = np.array([1, 2, 3, 4, 5, 6, 7, 8, 9, 10])
    # Extract a subarray from index 2 to index 5 (exclusive)
print(arr[2:5])
    # Extract every other element starting from index 1
print(arr[1::2]) # Output: [2, 4, 6, 8, 10]
    # Reverse the array
print(arr[::-1]) # Output: [10, 9, 8, 7, 6, 5, 4, 3, 2, 1]
```

Array Operation in Python

Python provides several built-in functions and methods for performing operations on arrays. Here are some common operations you can perform on arrays in Python:

Accessing Elements:

1. Indexing: Access individual elements by their index.

2. Slicing: Retrieve a portion of the array by specifying a range of indices.

Modifying Elements:

1. Assigning: Change the value of an element by assigning a new value to it.

2. Appending: Add elements to the end of an array using the append() method.

3. Inserting: Insert elements at a specific index using the insert() method.

4. Extending: Combine two arrays by appending the elements of one array to another using the extend() method.

5. Deleting: Remove elements from an array using the del statement or the remove() method.

Operations:

1. Length: Get the number of elements in the array using the len() function.

2. Concatenation: Join two arrays using the + operator.

3. Repetition: Repeat an array multiple times using the * operator.

4. Sorting: Sort the elements of an array using the sort() method or the sorted() function.

5. Searching: Find the index of a specific element in the array using the index() method.

6. Counting: Count the occurrences of a specific element in the array using the count() method.

7. Min and Max: Find the minimum and maximum values in the array using the min() and max() functions.

Here's an example that demonstrates some of these operations:

Code:

```python
# Creating an array
arr = [1, 2, 3, 4, 5]
# Accessing elements
print(arr[0]) # Output: 1
print(arr[2:4]) # Output: [3, 4]
# Modifying elements
arr[1] = 10
print(arr) # Output: [1, 10, 3, 4, 5]
arr.append(6)
print(arr) # Output: [1, 10, 3, 4, 5, 6]
arr.insert(2, 20)
print(arr) # Output: [1, 10, 20, 3, 4, 5, 6]
arr2 = [7, 8, 9]
arr.extend(arr2)
print(arr) # Output: [1, 10, 20, 3, 4, 5, 6, 7, 8, 9]
del arr[3]
print(arr) # Output: [1, 10, 20, 4, 5, 6, 7, 8, 9]
# Operations
print(len(arr)) # Output: 9
arr3 = arr + arr2
print(arr3) # Output: [1, 10, 20, 4, 5, 6, 7, 8, 9, 7, 8, 9]
arr4 = arr * 3
print(arr4) # Output: [1, 10, 20, 4, 5, 6, 7, 8, 9, 1, 10, 20, 4, 5, 6, 7, 8, 9, 1, 10, 20, 4, 5, 6, 7, 8, 9]
arr.sort()
print(arr) # Output: [1, 4, 5, 6, 7, 8, 9, 10, 20]
```

Statistical Operations on Arrays :

Python provides several libraries, such as NumPy and statistics, that offer functions for performing statistical operations on arrays. Here are some common statistical operations you can perform on arrays:

1. **Mean:** Calculate the average value of an array.

2. **Median:** Find the middle value of an array.

3. **Mode:** Determine the most frequently occurring value(s) in an array.

4. **Standard Deviation:** Measure the amount of variation or dispersion in an array.

5. **Variance:** Calculate the average of the squared differences from the mean.

6. **Range:** Find the difference between the maximum and minimum values in an array.

7. **Percentiles:** Calculate the value below which a given percentage of the data falls.

8. **Correlation:** Measure the relationship between two arrays.

9. **Covariance:** Measure how changes in one array correspond to changes in another array.

10. **Histogram:** Visualize the distribution of data by grouping values into bins.

Code:

```python
import numpy as np
# Creating an array
arr = np.array([1, 2, 3, 4, 5])
# Mean
mean = np.mean(arr)
print("Mean:", mean) # Output: 3.0
# Median
median = np.median(arr)
print("Median:", median) # Output: 3.0
# Mode
mode = np.mode(arr)
print("Mode:", mode) # Output: [1 2 3 4 5] - All elements are equally frequent
# Standard Deviation
std_dev = np.std(arr)
print("Standard Deviation:", std_dev) # Output: 1.4142135623730951
# Variance
variance = np.var(arr)
print("Variance:", variance) # Output: 2.0
# Range
range_val = np.ptp(arr)
print("Range:", range_val) # Output: 4
# Percentiles
percentile_25 = np.percentile(arr, 25)
print("25th Percentile:", percentile_25) # Output: 2.0
percentile_75 = np.percentile(arr, 75)
print("75th Percentile:", percentile_75) # Output: 4.0
# Correlation
arr2 = np.array([5, 4, 3, 2, 1])
correlation = np.corrcoef(arr, arr2)
print("Correlation:\n", correlation)
# Output: [[ 1. -1.]
# [-1. 1.]] - Perfect negative correlation
# Covariance
covariance = np.cov(arr, arr2)
print("Covariance:\n", covariance)
```

```python
# Output: [[ 2.5 -2.5]
#  [-2.5 2.5]]
    # Histogram
hist, bin_edges = np.histogram(arr, bins=[0, 2, 4, 6])
print("Histogram:", hist) # Output: [2 2 1]
print("Bin Edges:", bin_edges) # Output: [0 2 4 6]
```

TWELVE

FILE HANDLING IN PYTHON

File handling in Python refers to the process of reading from and writing to files using Python programming language. Python provides built-in functions and methods to handle files effectively.

Here are the basic steps involved in file handling:

1. Opening a file:

To start working with a file, you need to open it using the open() function. The open() function takes two parameters: the file path and the mode in which you want to open the file (read, write, append, etc.). For example, to open a file in read mode:

file = open("filename.txt", "r")

2. Reading from a file:

Once you have opened the file in read mode, you can use various methods to read its contents. The most common methods are read(), readline(), and readlines(). For example:

content = file.read() # Reads the entire file
line = file.readline() # Reads a single line
lines = file.readlines() # Reads all lines and returns a list

3. Writing to a file:

To write data to a file, you need to open it in write mode ("w") or append mode ("a"). Use the write() method to write data to the file. For example:

file = open("filename.txt", "w")
file.write("Hello, world!")
file.close()

4. Closing a file:

After you have finished working with a file, it's important to close it using the close() method. Closing a file releases the system resources associated with it. For example:

file.close()

It's good practice to close a file explicitly, but you can also use the with the statement, which automatically closes the file when you're done. For example:

with open("filename.txt", "r") as file:
content = file.read()

Do something with the file content
File is automatically closed outside the `with` block

Remember to handle exceptions appropriately when working with files, such as using try-except blocks or context managers (with statement), to ensure proper error handling and resource cleanup.

These are the basic concepts of file handling in Python. There are many more advanced techniques and methods available, such as file seek(), file tell(), working with binary files, CSV files, JSON files, etc. Python's os also provides additional file-related functionality for tasks like file/directory manipulation, file path operations, etc.

Code:

```python
# Open the file in read mode
file = open("example.txt", "r")
    # Read the contents of the file
content = file.read()
print(content)
    # Close the file
file.close()
```

In this example, we assume that there is a file named "example.txt" in the same directory as the Python script. The program opens the file using the open() function with the file name and "r" mode, which indicates that we want to read from the file. The resulting file object is stored in the variable file.

Next, we use the read() method of the file object to read the contents of the file. The read() method reads the entire contents of the file as a single string and stores it in the content variable. You can then perform any necessary operations on the content of the file.

Finally, we close the file using the close() method of the file object. It's important to close the file when you're done working with it to free up system resources and ensure that all changes are saved.

File Open Modes in Python

Python provides several modes for opening files using the open() function. Here are the most commonly used file open modes:

1. "r": Read mode (default). Opens the file for reading. If the file does not exist, it raises a FileNotFoundError.

2. "w": Write mode. Opens the file for writing. If the file exists, its contents are truncated (deleted). If the file does not exist, a new file is created.

3. "a": Append mode. Opens the file for appending. The file pointer is positioned at the end of the file, and any new data written to the file is added at the end. If the file does not exist, a new file is created.

4. "x": Exclusive creation mode. Opens the file for writing but raises a FileExistsError if the file already exists.

5. "b": Binary mode. Opens the file in binary mode, allowing you to read or write binary data.

6. "t": Text mode (default). Opens the file in text mode, allowing you to read or write text data (default encoding is platform-dependent).

Code:

```python
# Example of different file modes
# Read mode
file = open("example.txt", "r")
content = file.read()
print("Read mode content:")
print(content)
file.close()
    # Write mode
file = open("example.txt", "w")
file.write("This is some new content.")
```

```python
file.close()
    # Append mode
file = open("example.txt", "a")
file.write("\nThis content is appended.")
file.close()
    # Read mode again to see the updated content
file = open("example.txt", "r")
updated_content = file.read()
print("Updated content:")
print(updated_content)
file.close()
```

In this example, we assume there is a file named **"example.txt"** in the same directory as the Python script. The code first opens the file in read mode and reads its content using the read() method. It then prints the content. Next, the code opens the file in write mode and overwrites the content with the new string "This is some new content." After that, the code opens the file in append mode and adds the string "This content is appended." at the end of the file.

Finally, the code opens the file in read mode again and reads the updated content. It then prints the updated content to verify the changes made. Remember to close the file using the close() method to free up system resources and ensure that changes are saved.

readline method in Python:

The readline() method in Python is used to read a single line from a file. It reads characters from the current file position until it encounters a newline character ('\n') or reaches the end of the file.

The general syntax of the readline() method is as follows:

```python
line = file.readline()
```

Here, file represents the file object obtained by opening a file using the open() function. The readline() method reads the contents of the file up to and including the newline character. If the file does not have a newline character at the end of the line, the readline() method will read the entire line as a single string.

Code:

```python
    # Open the file in read mode
file = open("example.txt", "r")
    # Read the first line of the file
line1 = file.readline()
print("First line:", line1)
    # Read the second line of the file
line2 = file.readline()
print("Second line:", line2)
    # Close the file
file.close()
```

Output:

First line: Hello, World!

Second line: This is the second line.

In this example, the readline() method is called twice to read the first and second lines of the file, respectively. Each line is assigned to a separate variable (line1 and line2), and then printed to the console. Remember to close the file using the close() method when you're done working with it to free up system resources.

THIRTEEN
EXCEPTION HANDLING IN PYTHON

Exception handling in Python allows you to handle errors and unexpected situations that may occur during the execution of a program. By using exception handling, you can control how your program responds to errors, preventing it from crashing and providing meaningful error messages or alternative actions when something goes wrong. The primary components of exception handling in Python are the try, except, else, and finally blocks.

try block: The code that might raise an exception is placed inside the try block. If an exception occurs within this block, the control flow immediately jumps to the corresponding except block.

except block: If an exception is raised in the try block, the code inside the except block is executed. The except block defines the type of exception it can handle. You can specify multiple except blocks to handle different types of exceptions.

else block (optional): This block is executed only if no exception occurs in the try block. It is used to define code that should run when the try block runs successfully.

finally block (optional): The finally block contains code that is always executed, regardless of whether an exception occurred or not. It is often used to perform cleanup actions, such as closing files or releasing resources.

Syntax Error:

In Python, a syntax error is an error that occurs when the code violates the language's syntax rules. These errors are detected by the Python interpreter during the parsing phase before the program is executed. Syntax errors prevent the code from being compiled or interpreted successfully, and they must be fixed before the program can run.

1. Common causes of syntax errors include:
2. Incorrect spelling or typo in a keyword, function, variable, or any identifier.
3. Missing or mismatched parentheses, brackets, or curly braces.
4. Incorrect indentation or inconsistent use of tabs and spaces.
5. Improper use of operators or incorrect expression formation.
6. Missing or extra colons, commas, semicolons, or other punctuation marks.
7. Unclosed strings, comments, or multi-line statements.

Here's an example of a syntax error:

Code:

```
# Incorrect use of parentheses
print "Hello, World!"
```

 # Output: SyntaxError: Missing parentheses in call to 'print'. Did you mean print("Hello, World!")?

In this case, the error occurs because Python 3 requires parentheses when calling the print function, but the code uses the Python 2 syntax without parentheses.

Python's error messages for syntax errors typically provide helpful information that points to the location and type of the error, making it easier to identify and fix the issue.

Remember that syntax errors are distinct from logical errors, which occur when the code runs without any error but produces incorrect or unexpected results due to flawed logic or incorrect algorithms.

Built-in Exception in Python

In Python, there are several built-in exception classes that cover various types of errors and exceptional situations. These exceptions are used to handle errors gracefully and provide meaningful feedback to users when something goes wrong during the execution of a program.

Some common built-in exceptions in Python include:

1. SyntaxError: Raised when there is a syntax error in the code, violating Python's syntax rules.

2. IndentationError: Raised when there is an issue with the indentation in the code, usually caused by inconsistent use of tabs and spaces.

3. TypeError: Raised when an operation or function is applied to an object of an inappropriate type.

4. ValueError: Raised when a function receives an argument of the correct type but an inappropriate value.

5. NameError: Raised when a local or global name is not found or not defined.

6. IndexError: Raised when trying to access an index that is out of range in a sequence (e.g., list, tuple, string).

7. KeyError: Raised when trying to access a non-existing key in a dictionary.

8. ZeroDivisionError: Raised when trying to divide by zero.

9. FileNotFoundError: Raised when attempting to open or access a file that does not exist.

10. IOError: Raised when an I/O (input/output) operation fails.

11. ImportError: Raised when an import statement fails to find and load a module.

12. AttributeError: Raised when an attribute reference or assignment fails.

13. RuntimeError: A generic error that can be raised when no other specific exception fits the situation.

14. OverflowError: Raised when an arithmetic operation exceeds the limit of a numeric type.

15. StopIteration: Raised by the next() function when there are no more items to be returned by an iterator.

16. KeyboardInterrupt: Raised when the user interrupts the program's execution, usually by pressing Ctrl+C.

These are just a few examples of the many built-in exceptions in Python. You can catch these exceptions using the try, except, else, and finally blocks to handle errors gracefully and control the flow of your program in case something unexpected occurs. Additionally, you can create custom exception classes by subclassing existing exceptions or the Exception class to handle specific exceptional situations in your code.

Raise Statment in Python:

In Python, the raise statement is used to explicitly raise an exception during the execution of a program. It allows you to signal that an exceptional situation has occurred and provides a way to handle specific errors or exceptional cases in your code. When you raise an exception using the raise statement, the program flow is disrupted, and the exception is propagated up the call stack until it is caught by an appropriate except block or until the program terminates if it's not caught.

The basic syntax of the raise statement is as follows:

raise [ExceptionType[(args)]]

Here's a breakdown of the components:

ExceptionType: This is the type of exception you want to raise. It can be any built-in exception (e.g., ValueError, TypeError, ZeroDivisionError) or a custom exception class that you have defined by subclassing an existing exception or the base Exception class.

(args): This part is optional and is used to pass additional arguments to the exception class's constructor if needed. Not all exceptions require additional arguments.

Example using a built-in exception:

Code:

```
    def divide_numbers(a, b):
if b == 0:
raise ValueError("Division by zero is not allowed.")
return a / b
    try:
result = divide_numbers(10, 0)
except ValueError as e:
print(f"Error: {e}")
else:
print("The result of the division is:", result)
finally:
print("Exception handling is complete.")
```

Example using a custom exception:

Code:

In the first example, the raise statement is used to raise a ValueError when attempting to divide by zero. In the second example, a custom exception CustomError is raised explicitly within the some_function().

When using the raise statement, it's important to consider what kind of exception to raise and ensure that the appropriate except block is available to catch the raised exception and handle it accordingly.

```
    class CustomError(Exception):
pass
    def some_function():
# Some condition that triggers the custom exception
raise CustomError("This is a custom error.")
    try:
some_function()
except CustomError as ce:
print(f"Custom Error: {ce}")
finally:
print("Exception handling is complete.")
```

In the first example, the raise statement is used to raise a ValueError when attempting to divide by zero. In the second example, a custom exception CustomError is raised explicitly within the some_function().

When using the raise statement, it's important to consider what kind of an exception to raise and ensure that the appropriate except block is available to catch the raised exception and handle it accordingly.

Steps of Exception Handling:

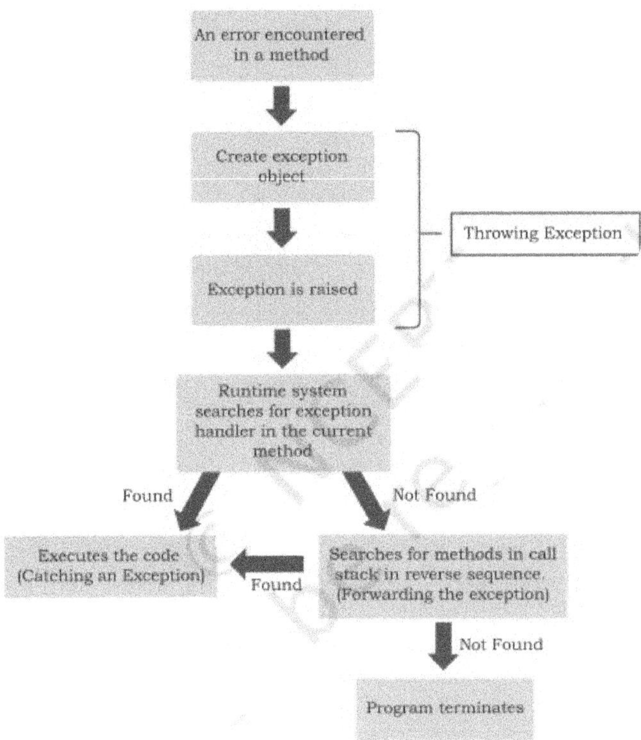

via NCERT BOOK

Need for Exception Handling

Exception handling is being used not only in Python programming but in most programming languages like C++, Java, Ruby, etc. It is a useful technique that helps in capturing runtime errors and handling them so as to avoid the program getting crashed. Following are some of the important points regarding exceptions and their handling:

• Python categorizes exceptions into distinct types so that specific exception handlers (code to handle that particular exception) can be created for each type.

• Exception handlers separate the main logic of the program from the error detection and correction code. The segment of code where there is any possibility of error or exception, is placed inside one block. The code to be executed in case the exception has occurred is placed inside another block. These statements for detection and reporting the exception do not affect the main logic of the program.

• The compiler or interpreter keeps track of the exact position where the error has occurred.

• Exception handling can be done for both user-defined and built-in exceptions.

FOURTEEN
DATA HANDLING USING PANDAS -I

Pandas is a popular open-source library in Python for data manipulation and analysis. It provides easy-to-use data structures and data analysis tools, making it a powerful tool for working with structured data. The name "Pandas" is derived from the term "panel data," which refers to multidimensional structured data sets.

Key features of pandas include:

DataFrame: The DataFrame is the primary data structure in pandas. It is a two-dimensional tabular data structure similar to a spreadsheet or SQL table. DataFrames allow you to store and manipulate data in rows and columns.

Series: A Series is a one-dimensional array-like object in pandas, consisting of a sequence of data values with an associated index. A DataFrame is essentially a collection of Series objects.

Data Manipulation: Pandas provides a wide range of functions and methods for filtering, cleaning, transforming, and aggregating data. It allows you to perform tasks like selecting specific rows or columns, handling missing data, merging and joining datasets, and much more.

I/O Operations: Pandas supports reading and writing data from various file formats such as CSV, Excel, SQL databases, and more.

Time Series Functionality: Pandas has built-in support for working with time-series data, making it easier to handle date and time data.

Broadcasting: Pandas supports element-wise operations, similar to NumPy arrays, enabling you to perform operations on entire data structures efficiently.

To use pandas, you first need to install it, which can be done using the following command in your Python environment:

pip install pandas

Once installed, you can import pandas in your Python script or interactive session using:

import pandas as pd

With pandas, you can efficiently work with datasets, perform data analysis, and prepare data for further processing or visualization. It has become an essential tool in the data science ecosystem due to its ease of use and powerful capabilities.

You may think what the need for Pandas is when NumPy can be used for data analysis. Following are some of **the differences between Pandas and Numpy:**

1. A Numpy array requires homogeneous data, while a Pandas DataFrame can have different data types (float, int, string, datetime, etc.).

2. Pandas have a simpler interface for operations like file loading, plotting, selection, joining, GROUP BY, which come very handy in data-processing applications.

3. Pandas DataFrames (with column names) make it very easy to keep track of data.

4. Pandas is used when data is in Tabular Format, whereas Numpy is used for numeric array based data manipulation.

Data Structure in Python

In pandas, the primary data structures are the Series and the DataFrame. These data structures are built on top of NumPy arrays and provide powerful tools for working with structured data. Let's explore each of these data structures:

1. Series:

A Series is a one-dimensional labeled array that can hold data of any type (integers, floats, strings, etc.). It is similar to a NumPy array but with an associated index that labels each element. The basic syntax to create a Series is as follows:

Code:

import pandas as pd

 # Creating a Series from a list

data = [10, 20, 30, 40, 50]

series = pd.Series(data)

Output:

  0 10

1 20

2 30

3 40

4 50

dtype: int64

2. DataFrame:

A dataframe is a two-dimensional tabular data structure, similar to a spreadsheet or SQL table. It consists of rows and columns, where each column can have a different data type. DataFrames can be created from various sources like dictionaries, lists of lists, NumPy arrays, and more. The basic syntax to create a DataFrame is as follows:

Code :

import pandas as pd

 # Creating a DataFrame from a dictionary

data = {

'Name': ['Alice', 'Bob', 'Charlie', 'David'],

'Age': [25, 30, 35, 40],

'City': ['New York', 'San Francisco', 'London', 'Tokyo']

}

  df = pd.DataFrame(data)

  Output:

  Name Age City

0 Alice 25 New York

1 Bob 30 San Francisco

2 Charlie 35 London

3 David 40 Tokyo

DataFrames provide various methods and functions to perform data manipulation, filtering, merging, grouping, and more. They are widely used in data analysis and data preparation tasks.

Both Series and DataFrames support indexing, slicing, and advanced data manipulation techniques. They are the backbone of the pandas library and form the foundation for most data analysis workflows in Python.

Creation of Series from NumPy Arrays:

Creating a pandas Series from a NumPy array is straightforward. Since pandas are built on top of NumPy, it seamlessly integrates with NumPy arrays.

Here's how you can create a Series from a NumPy array:

Code:

```python
import numpy as np
import pandas as pd
# Creating a NumPy array
numpy_array = np.array([10, 20, 30, 40, 50])
# Creating a pandas Series from the NumPy array
series = pd.Series(numpy_array)
print(series)
```

Output:

```
0 10
1 20
2 30
3 40
4 50
dtype: int64
```

As you can see, the resulting Series is indexed with default integer labels (0 to n-1, where n is the number of elements in the array). The data type of the elements in the Series is inferred from the NumPy array.

You can also provide custom index labels when creating the Series.

For example:

```python
import numpy as np
import pandas as pd
# Creating a NumPy array
numpy_array = np.array([10, 20, 30, 40, 50])
# Creating a pandas Series with custom index labels
index_labels = ['A', 'B', 'C', 'D', 'E']
series = pd.Series(numpy_array, index=index_labels)
print(series)
```

Output:

```
A 10
B 20
C 30
D 40
E 50
dtype: int64
```

In this case, the Series is indexed with the provided custom labels 'A', 'B', 'C', 'D', and 'E'. The association of data with labels is a powerful feature of pandas that allows for more meaningful and flexible data manipulation and analysis.

Creation of Series from Scalar Values:

In Python, you can create a Series from scalar values using the pandas library. The Series is a one-dimensional labeled array, similar to a list or an array, but with additional functionalities. Here's how you can create a Series from scalar values:

```python
import pandas as pd
```

```
# Create a Series from a single scalar value
scalar_value = 42
series = pd.Series(scalar_value)
    print(series)
    Output:
    0 42
dtype: int64
```

By default, when creating a Series from a scalar value, pandas automatically assign an index to the value. In this case, the index is 0. The data type of the Series is inferred from the scalar value.

Creation of Series from Dictionary:

In Python, you can create a Series from a dictionary using the pandas library. When creating a Series from a dictionary, the dictionary keys will become the index labels, and the dictionary values will become the data values in the Series. Here's how you can do it:

```
import pandas as pd
# Create a dictionary
data_dict = {
'A': 10,
'B': 20,
'C': 30,
'D': 40
}
    # Create a Series from the dictionary
series = pd.Series(data_dict)
    print(series)
    Output:
    A 10
B 20
C 30
D 40
dtype: int64
```

As you can see, the keys from the dictionary ('A', 'B', 'C', 'D') have become the index labels, and the corresponding values (10, 20, 30, 40) have become the data values in the Series.

You can also pass additional arguments to the pd.Series() function to specify custom index labels or data types, if needed. For example:

```
import pandas as pd
# Create a dictionary
data_dict = {
'A': 10,
'B': 20,
'C': 30,
'D': 40
}
    # Create a Series from the dictionary with custom index labels
index_labels = ['D', 'C', 'B', 'A']
series = pd.Series(data_dict, index=index_labels)
    print(series)
```

```
Output:
   D 40
C 30
B 20
A 10
dtype: int64
```

Accessing Elements of a Series :

In pandas, a Series is a one-dimensional labeled array capable of holding any data type. You can think of it as a column in a spreadsheet or a dictionary-like object. To access elements of a Series, you can use various methods and indexing techniques. Here are some common ways to access elements in a pandas Series:

1. Using numerical indexing:

```
Code:
import pandas as pd
    # Create a Series
data = [10, 20, 30, 40, 50]
series = pd.Series(data)
    # Access the element at index 2 (which is 30)
element = series[2]
print(element)
    Output:
30
```

2. Using label-based indexing (index names):

```
Code :
import pandas as pd
    # Create a Series with custom index names
data = [10, 20, 30, 40, 50]
index_names = ['A', 'B', 'C', 'D', 'E']
series = pd.Series(data, index=index_names)
    # Access the element with label 'C' (which is 30)
element = series['D']
print(element)
    Output:
40
```

3. Using a list of numerical indices:

```
Code:
import pandas as pd
    # Create a Series
data = [10, 20, 30, 40, 50]
series = pd.Series(data)
```

```
# Access multiple elements using a list of indices (returns a new Series)
elements = series[[0, 2, 4]]
print(elements)
    Output:
    0 10
2 30
4 50
dtype: int64
```

Slicing in Pandas:

In pandas, slicing is the process of extracting a specific subset of data from a Series or DataFrame. It allows you to select rows, columns, or both based on their positions or labels. Slicing is a fundamental operation in pandas and is widely used for data manipulation and analysis.

Here are the key aspects of slicing in pandas:

1. Slicing Rows:

You can use numerical indices or label-based indexing to select a range of rows from a DataFrame or Series. Slicing with numerical indices is done using the .iloc indexer, while slicing with label-based indexing is done using the .loc indexer.

2. Slicing Columns:

To select specific columns from a DataFrame, you can use their column names as a list inside double square brackets ([[...]]). You can also use the .loc indexer with a colon (:) to select all rows and specific columns based on their labels.

3. Slicing Both Rows and Columns:

By combining row and column slicing, you can select a specific subset of data from a DataFrame. Row and column slicing can be done using both numerical indices and label-based indexing.

4. Conditional Slicing:

Conditional slicing allows you to select rows from a DataFrame that satisfy certain conditions based on the values in one or more columns.

Here are some examples of slicing in pandas:

Code:

```
import pandas as pd
# Create a sample DataFrame
data = {
'Name': ['Alice', 'Bob', 'Charlie', 'David', 'Eva'],
'Age': [25, 30, 35, 40, 45],
'City': ['New York', 'London', 'Paris', 'Tokyo', 'Sydney']
}
df = pd.DataFrame(data)
    # Slicing Rows using numerical indices
sliced_rows = df.iloc[1:4] # Selects rows with indices 1, 2, and 3
print("Sliced Rows using numerical indices:")
print(sliced_rows)
print()
    # Slicing Rows using label-based indexing
sliced_rows_labels = df.loc[1:3] # Selects rows with labels 1, 2, and 3
print("Sliced Rows using label-based indexing:")
print(sliced_rows_labels)
```

```
print()
    # Slicing Columns
sliced_columns = df[['Name', 'Age']] # Selects only 'Name' and 'Age' columns
print("Sliced Columns:")
print(sliced_columns)
print()
    # Slicing Rows and Columns using label-based indexing
sliced_subset = df.loc[1:3, ['Name', 'City']] # Selects rows with labels 1, 2, and 3, and columns 'Name' and 'City'
print("Sliced Rows and Columns using label-based indexing:")
print(sliced_subset)
print()
    # Conditional Slicing
sliced_conditional = df[df['Age'] > 30] # Selects rows where Age is greater than 30
print("Conditional Slicing:")
print(sliced_conditional)
```

Output:
    Sliced Rows using numerical indices:
Name Age City
1 Bob 30 London
2 Charlie 35 Paris
3 David 40 Tokyo
    Sliced Rows using label-based indexing:
Name Age City
1 Bob 30 London
2 Charlie 35 Paris
3 David 40 Tokyo
    Sliced Columns:
Name Age
0 Alice 25
1 Bob 30
2 Charlie 35
3 David 40
4 Eva 45
    Sliced Rows and Columns using label-based indexing:
Name City
1 Bob London
2 Charlie Paris
3 David Tokyo
    Conditional Slicing:
Name Age City
2 Charlie 35 Paris
3 David 40 Tokyo
4 Eva 45 Sydney

In this code, we first create a DataFrame using pandas with some sample data. Then, we demonstrate different types of slicing operations using both numerical indices and label-based indexing. The output displays the sliced subsets of the DataFrame based on the slicing conditions.

Creation of DataFrame from NumPy ndarrays:

Creating a DataFrame from NumPy ndarrays is a common operation in data analysis and manipulation using Python. To do this, you'll need to have NumPy and pandas installed. If you don't have them yet, you can install them using pip:

pip install numpy pandas

Once you have NumPy and pandas installed, you can proceed with creating a DataFrame from NumPy ndarrays. Here's a step-by-step guide:

Step 1: Import the necessary libraries.

import numpy as np

import pandas as pd

Step 2: Create your NumPy ndarrays with the data you want to include in the DataFrame.

For example, let's create two NumPy arrays representing columns of data:

Code:

```
# Example NumPy ndarrays
names = np.array(["Alice", "Bob", "Charlie", "David"])
ages = np.array([25, 30, 22, 28])
scores = np.array([85, 92, 78, 88])
```

Step 3: Combine the ndarrays into a dictionary with column names as keys and ndarrays as values.

Code:

```
# Combine ndarrays into a dictionary
data = {
"Name": names,
"Age": ages,
"Score": scores
}
```

Step 4: Convert the dictionary into a pandas DataFrame.

Code:

```
# Convert dictionary to DataFrame
df = pd.DataFrame(data)
```

Step 5: Now you have your DataFrame ready. You can print it or perform various operations on it.

print(df)

Output:

```
   Name Age Score
0 Alice 25 85
1 Bob 30 92
2 Charlie 22 78
3 David 28 88
```

That's it! You've successfully created a DataFrame from NumPy ndarrays. You can use this approach for more complex data with multiple columns and rows. The DataFrame provides powerful tools for data manipulation, analysis, and visualization.

Creation of DataFrame from List of Dictionaries:

Creating a DataFrame from a list of dictionaries is another common way to create a DataFrame in pandas. Each dictionary in the list represents a row in the DataFrame, where the keys of the dictionaries become the column names, and the values become the data in the corresponding columns.

Here's how you can do it:

Step 1: Import the necessary libraries.

Step 2: Create a list of dictionaries, where each dictionary represents a row of data.

Step 3: Convert the list of dictionaries into a pandas DataFrame.

Step 4: Now you have your DataFrame ready. You can print it or perform various operations on it.

Code:

```python
import pandas as pd
# Example list of dictionaries
data_list = [
{"Name": "Alice", "Age": 25, "Score": 85},
{"Name": "Bob", "Age": 30, "Score": 92},
{"Name": "Charlie", "Age": 22, "Score": 78},
{"Name": "David", "Age": 28, "Score": 88}
]
    # Convert list of dictionaries to DataFrame
df = pd.DataFrame(data_list)
print(df)
```

Output:

```
Name Age Score
0 Alice 25 85
1 Bob 30 92
2 Charlie 22 78
3 David 28 88
```

That's it! You've successfully created a DataFrame from a list of dictionaries. This method is useful when you have data in a structured format, such as frCodom JSON files or database queries, and want to quickly convert it into a DataFrame for further analysis and manipulation using pandas.

Creation of DataFrame from Dictionary of Lists :

Creating a DataFrame from a dictionary of lists is another common method in pandas. Each key-value pair in the dictionary represents a column in the DataFrame, where the key becomes the column name, and the list associated with that key becomes the data in the corresponding column.

Here's how you can do it:

Step 1: Import the necessary libraries.

Step 2: Create a dictionary where keys are column names, and values are lists containing data for each column.

Step 3: Convert the dictionary into a pandas DataFrame.

Step 4: Now you have your DataFrame ready. You can print it or perform various operations on it.

Code:

```python
import pandas as pd
# Example dictionary of lists
data_dict = {
"Name": ["Aliza", "Rahul", "Concept", "Classes"],
"Age": [25, 30, 22, 28],
"Score": [85, 92, 78, 88]
}
# Convert dictionary of lists to DataFrame
df = pd.DataFrame(data_dict)
print(df)
```

Output:

```
     Name Age Score
0 Aliza 25 85
1 Rahul 30 92
2 Concept 22 78
3 Classes 28 88
```

Operations on rows and columns in DataFrames:

A) Adding a New Column to a DataFrame :
    To add a new column to a DataFrame in pandas, you can simply assign a new list or NumPy array to a new column name. The new column will be automatically added to the DataFrame with the provided data.
    Let's assume you already have a DataFrame, and you want to add a new column to it.
    Code:

```python
import pandas as pd
# Example DataFrame
data = {
"Name": ["Alice", "Bob", "Charlie", "David"],
"Age": [25, 30, 22, 28],
"Score": [85, 92, 78, 88]
}
    df = pd.DataFrame(data)
# Adding a new column "Grade" to the DataFrame
grades = ["A", "A+", "B", "B+"]
df["Grade"] = grades
# Adding a new column "Pass/Fail" based on the "Score" column
df["Pass/Fail"] = df["Score"] >= 80
```

Output:

```
Name Age Score Grade Pass/Fail
0 Alice 25 85 A True
1 Bob 30 92 A+ True
2 Charlie 22 78 B False
3 David 28 88 B+ True
```

    The "Pass/Fail" column has been added based on whether the "Score" is greater than or equal to 80.
    Remember that when you assign a new column, the length of the data you provide should match the number of rows in the DataFrame. If it doesn't match, pandas will raise an error.

Accessing DataFrames Elements through Indexing:

In pandas, you can access elements in a DataFrame through indexing. There are multiple ways to achieve this, and I'll cover the most commonly used methods:
    1. Accessing Columns: To access a specific column in the DataFrame, you can use either dot notation or square brackets with the column name.
    Code:

```python
import pandas as pd
    # Create a sample DataFrame
data = {
"Name": ["Aadil", "Ruheen", "Kumkum", "Zeenat"],
```

```
"Age": [25, 30, 22, 28],
"Score": [85, 92, 78, 88]
}
    df = pd.DataFrame(data)
    # Access the "Name" column using dot notation
names = df.Name
    # Access the "Age" column using square brackets
ages = df['Age']
    print(names)
print(ages)
    Output:
0 Aadil
1 Ruheen
2 Kumkum
3 Zeenat
Name: Name, dtype: object
0 25
1 30
2 22
3 28
Name: Age, dtype: int64
```

Data elements in a DataFrame can be accessed using indexing.

There are two ways of indexing Dataframes :

1. Label-based indexing:

Label-based indexing in pandas is accomplished using the .loc attribute. It allows you to access data in a DataFrame by specifying row labels and column labels, rather than using integer-based indexing like .iloc.

The general syntax for label-based indexing using .loc is as follows:

df.loc[row_label, column_label]

```
    Code:
    import pandas as pd
    # Create a sample DataFrame
data = {
"Name": ["Aadil", "Abhay", "Chirag", "David"],
"Age": [25, 30, 22, 28],
"Score": [85, 92, 78, 88]
}
    df = pd.DataFrame(data)
    # Set the "Name" column as the index for label-based indexing
df.set_index("Name", inplace=True)
    # Accessing data using label-based indexing
Aadil_row = df.loc["Aadil"]
david_score = df.loc["David", "Score"]
    print(Aadil_row)
print("David Score is : ",david_score)
    Output:
 Age 25
```

Score 85
Name: Aadil, dtype: int64
David Score is: 88

In the example above, we first set the "Name" column as the index of the DataFrame using set_index(). This step is essential for label-based indexing to work on the "Name" column.

After setting the index, we use .loc to access data. df.loc["Aadil"] retrieves the row with the label "Aadil," and df.loc["David", "Score"] retrieves the value in the "Score" column for the row with the label "David."

Label-based indexing is more explicit and easier to use when you have meaningful row and column labels. It is particularly useful when working with DataFrames that have non-integer indices, such as dates, categories, or other unique identifiers.

2. Boolean Indexing:

Boolean indexing is a powerful feature in pandas that allows you to filter a DataFrame based on a condition and retrieve the rows that meet that condition. It involves using boolean (True/False) masks to select rows that satisfy a given criterion.

Here's how boolean indexing works in pandas:

Code:

```
import pandas as pd
    # Create a sample DataFrame
data = {
"Name": ["Alice", "Bob", "Charlie", "David"],
"Age": [25, 30, 22, 28],
"Score": [85, 92, 78, 88]
}
    df = pd.DataFrame(data)
    # Boolean indexing example: Select rows where Age is greater than 25
age_condition = df['Age'] > 25
result_df = df[age_condition]
    print(result_df)
    Output:
Name Age Score
1 Bob 30 92
3 David 28 88
```

n the example above, we create a DataFrame with three columns: "Name", "Age", and "Score". We then use boolean indexing to filter and select rows where the "Age" is greater than 25.

The steps for boolean indexing are as follows:

We define a condition using a comparison or any other logical operation on one of the DataFrame columns. In this case, the condition is df['Age'] > 25, which creates a boolean mask with True for rows where the "Age" is greater than 25 and False for rows where it is not.

We use this boolean mask to index the DataFrame using square brackets. When we pass the boolean mask age_condition inside the brackets df[age_condition], pandas selects only the rows where the condition is True, effectively filtering out the rows that don't meet the condition.

Code:

```
import pandas as pd
    # Create a sample DataFrame
data = {
"Name": ["Aadil", "Abhay", "Chirag", "David"],
"Age": [25, 30, 22, 28],
"Score": [85, 92, 78, 88]
```

```
}
    df = pd.DataFrame(data)
    # Boolean indexing example: Select rows where Age is greater than 25
age_condition = df['Age'] > 25
boolean_mask = df['Age'] > 25
    print("Boolean Mask:")
print(boolean_mask)
    Output:
Boolean Mask:
0 False
1 True
2 False
3 True
Name: Age, dtype: bool
```

In this example, boolean_mask contains a Series of boolean values (True/False), where each value corresponds to whether the condition df['Age'] > 25 is true or false for each row in the DataFrame.

Joining, Merging, and Concatenation of DataFrames:

In data manipulation with pandas, joining, merging, and concatenation are important operations when working with DataFrames. They allow you to combine data from different sources, perform relational database-like operations, and concatenate data along different axes. Let's go through each operation one by one:

Concatenation: Concatenation simply means stacking DataFrames on top of each other (vertically) or side by side (horizontally). The **pd.concat()** function is used for this operation.

1. Vertical Concatenation:

To stack DataFrames vertically, they must have the same columns. The new DataFrame will have all the rows from the input DataFrames.

Code:

```
import pandas as pd
    # Sample DataFrames
df1 = pd.DataFrame({'A': [1, 2, 3], 'B': [4, 5, 6]})
df2 = pd.DataFrame({'A': [7, 8, 9], 'B': [10, 11, 12]})
    # Vertical concatenation
result_vertical = pd.concat([df1, df2], axis=0)
print(result_vertical)
    Output:
A B
0 1 4
1 2 5
2 3 6
0 7 10
1 8 11
2 9 12
```

2. Horizontal Concatenation: |

To stack DataFrames horizontally, they must have the same number of rows. The new DataFrame will have all the columns from the input DataFrames.

Code:

```
import pandas as pd
```

```
    # Sample DataFrames
df1 = pd.DataFrame({'A': [1, 2, 3], 'B': [4, 5, 6]})
df2 = pd.DataFrame({'C': [7, 8, 9], 'D': [10, 11, 12]})
    # Horizontal concatenation
result_horizontal = pd.concat([df1, df2], axis=1)
print(result_horizontal)
    Output:
A B C D
0 1 4 7 10
1 2 5 8 11
2 3 6 9 12
```

1. Merging in DataFrames :

Merging is similar to SQL joins and allows you to combine DataFrames based on a common column (key). The **pd.merge()** function is used for this operation.

```
    Code:
    import pandas as pd
    # Sample DataFrames
df1 = pd.DataFrame({'ID': [1, 2, 3], 'Name': ['Aadil', 'khan', 'Divyanshi']})
df2 = pd.DataFrame({'ID': [2, 3, 4], 'Age': [25, 30, 22]})
    # Merge based on the 'ID' column
result = pd.merge(df1, df2, on='ID', how='inner')
print(result)
    Output:
ID Name Age
0 2 khan 25
1 3 Divyanshi 30
```

2. Joining in DataFrames :

Joining is a convenient method to combine DataFrames based on their indices. It is a specific case of merging where the keys are the indices. The DataFrame.join() method is used for this operation.

```
    Code:
import pandas as pd
    # Sample DataFrames
df1 = pd.DataFrame({'A': [1, 2, 3], 'B': [4, 5, 6]}, index=['x', 'y', 'z'])
df2 = pd.DataFrame({'C': [7, 8, 9], 'D': [10, 11, 12]}, index=['y', 'z', 'w'])
    # Join based on indices
result = df1.join(df2, how='inner')
print(result)
    Output:
A B C D
y 2 5 7 10
z 3 6 8 11
```

n this example, we perform an inner join, which only includes rows where the index exists in both DataFrames.

Keep in mind that when joining or merging DataFrames, there are different types of joins (e.g., inner join, left join, right join, and outer join), and you can specify the appropriate one based on your needs.

It's crucial to understand the differences between concatenation, merging, and joining, as they have different use cases and requirements.

Difference between Pandas Series and NumPy Arrays

Feature	Pandas Series	NumPy Arrays
Data Structure	1-dimensional labeled array	n-dimensional homogeneous array
Indexing	Can have custom row labels (index)	Always uses implicit integer index
Data Types	Supports mixed data types	Supports homogeneous data types
Operations	Provides additional functionalities	Focused on array-oriented operations
Missing Values	Can represent missing data (NaN)	Does not have built-in missing data
Ease of Use	Designed for ease of data analysis	Designed for numerical computations
Labeling	Can be labeled and indexed by names	Indexed using integer positions
Size Flexibility	Can dynamically resize the Series	Size is fixed after creation
Memory Usage	May use more memory for labels	Generally more memory efficient
Performance	Slightly slower for numerical tasks	Faster for numerical computations

FIFTEEN
DATA HANDLING USING PANDAS – II

In this chapter, we will be working with more advanced features of DataFrame like sorting data, answering analytical questions using the data, cleaning data and applying different useful functions on the data. Below is the example data on which we will be applying the advanced features of Pandas.

Case Study :

Code:

```
    import pandas as pd
    # Sample data for 10 students
data = {
'Student_ID': [1, 2, 3, 4, 5, 6, 7, 8, 9, 10],
'English': [85, 78, 92, 88, 70, 95, 83, 76, 89, 80],
'Science': [90, 85, 78, 91, 82, 76, 88, 93, 84, 79],
'Maths': [76, 84, 92, 88, 78, 87, 81, 90, 85, 82],
'SST': [87, 89, 81, 78, 94, 85, 90, 76, 83, 88]
}
    # Create a DataFrame
df = pd.DataFrame(data)
    # Display the DataFrame
print(df)
    Output:
Student_ID English Science Maths SST
0 1 85 90 76 87
1 2 78 85 84 89
2 3 92 78 92 81
3 4 88 91 88 78
4 5 70 82 78 94
5 6 95 76 87 85
6 7 83 88 81 90
7 8 76 93 90 76
8 9 89 84 85 83
9 10 80 79 82 88
```

Descriptive Statistics :

re used to get some basic idea about the data. In this section, we will be discussing descriptive statistical methods that can be applied to a DataFrame. **These are max, min, count, sum, mean, median, mode, quartiles, and variance.** In each case, we will consider the above-created DataFrame df.

In pandas, you can easily compute descriptive statistics for a DataFrame using various **built-in functions**. Here are some common descriptive statistics functions in pandas:

1. describe(): This function provides a summary of the central tendency, dispersion, and shape of the distribution of a DataFrame. It returns statistics like count, mean, standard deviation, minimum, 25th percentile (Q1), median (50th percentile), 75th percentile (Q3), and maximum.

2. mean(): Computes the mean (average) value of each column in the DataFrame.

3. median(): Calculates the median (middle value) of each column.

4. mode(): Returns the mode (most frequently occurring value) of each column.

5. std(): Computes the standard deviation of each column.

6. min(), max(): Returns the minimum and maximum values of each column.

7. count(): Gives the count of non-null values for each column.

8. quantile(q): Calculates the qth percentile of each column, where q should be a float between 0 and 1.

9. sum(): Computes the sum of each column.

10. var(): Calculates the variance of each column.

Code:

```python
import pandas as pd
    # Sample data for 10 students
data = {
'English': [85, 78, 92, 88, 70, 95, 83, 76, 89, 80],
'Science': [90, 85, 78, 91, 82, 76, 88, 93, 84, 79],
'Maths': [76, 84, 92, 88, 78, 87, 81, 90, 85, 82],
'SST': [87, 89, 81, 78, 94, 85, 90, 76, 83, 88]
}
    # Create a DataFrame
df = pd.DataFrame(data)
    # Use describe() to get a summary of descriptive statistics
print(df.describe())
    # Individual descriptive statistics functions
print("Mean:")
print(df.mean())
    print("\nMedian:")
print(df.median())
    print("\nMode:")
print(df.mode().iloc[0]) # In case there are multiple modes, this will return the first one.
    print("\nStandard Deviation:")
print(df.std())
    print("\nMinimum Values:")
print(df.min())
    print("\nMaximum Values:")
print(df.max())
```

```python
    print("\nCount of Non-Null Values:")
print(df.count())
    print("\n25th Percentile (Q1):")
print(df.quantile(0.25))
    print("\n75th Percentile (Q3):")
print(df.quantile(0.75))
    print("\nSum:")
print(df.sum())
    print("\nVariance:")
print(df.var())
```

Output:

```
English Science Maths SST
count 10.000000 10.000000 10.000000 10.000000
mean 83.600000 84.600000 84.300000 85.100000
std 7.734483 5.853774 5.143496 5.626327
min 70.000000 76.000000 76.000000 76.000000
25% 78.500000 79.750000 81.250000 81.500000
50% 84.000000 84.500000 84.500000 86.000000
75% 88.750000 89.500000 87.750000 88.750000
max 95.000000 93.000000 92.000000 94.000000
    Mean:
English 83.6
Science 84.6
Maths 84.3
SST 85.1
dtype: float64
    Median:
English 84.0
Science 84.5
Maths 84.5
SST 86.0
dtype: float64
    Mode:
English 70
Science 76
Maths 76
SST 76
Name: 0, dtype: int64
    Standard Deviation:
English 7.734483
Science 5.853774
Maths 5.143496
SST 5.626327
dtype: float64
    Minimum Values:
English 70
Science 76
Maths 76
```

SST 76
dtype: int64
   Maximum Values:
English 95
Science 93
Maths 92
SST 94
dtype: int64
   Count of Non-Null Values:
English 10
Science 10
Maths 10
SST 10
dtype: int64
   25th Percentile (Q1):
English 78.50
Science 79.75
Maths 81.25
SST 81.50
Name: 0.25, dtype: float64
   75th Percentile (Q3):
English 88.75
Science 89.50
Maths 87.75
SST 88.75
Name: 0.75, dtype: float64
   Sum:
English 836
Science 846
Maths 843
SST 851
dtype: int64
   Variance:
English 59.822222
Science 34.266667
Maths 26.455556
SST 31.655556
dtype: float64

Sorting in DataFrame :

Sorting in a DataFrame refers to arranging the rows of the DataFrame in a specific order based on the values in one or more columns. Sorting is a common operation in data analysis, as it allows you to organize data in a meaningful way and gain insights into the dataset.

In pandas, the primary function used for sorting DataFrames is sort_values(). It allows you to sort the rows based on the values of one or more columns. The sort_values() function creates a new DataFrame with the rows rearranged in the specified order, leaving the original DataFrame unchanged.

Here's a summary of the sort_values() function:

DataFrame.sort_values(by, axis=0, ascending=True, inplace=False, na_position='last', ignore_index=False)

by: The column or list of columns by which you want to sort the DataFrame.

axis: The axis along which to sort. By default, axis=0, which means sorting rows. Use axis=1 for sorting columns.

ascending: A boolean or list of booleans indicating whether to sort in ascending (True) or descending (False) order. If sorting by multiple columns, you can use a list of booleans to specify the sorting order for each column.

inplace: If True, the DataFrame will be modified in place, and the sorted order will be applied to the original DataFrame.

na_position: Specifies where the missing values (NaNs) should be placed during sorting. By default, 'last', meaning NaNs are placed at the end. You can also use 'first' to place NaNs at the beginning.

ignore_index: If True, the resulting DataFrame will have a new index range from 0 to n-1, where n is the number of rows in the DataFrame. If False, the original index will be retained in the sorted DataFrame.

Code:

```python
import pandas as pd
# Sample data for 5 students
data = {
'Student_ID': [1, 2, 3, 4, 5],
'English': [85, 78, 92, 88, 70],
'Science': [90, 85, 78, 91, 82],
'Maths': [76, 84, 92, 88, 78],
'SST': [87, 89, 81, 78, 94]
}
# Create a DataFrame
df = pd.DataFrame(data)
# Sorting by English marks in ascending order
sorted_df = df.sort_values(by=['English', 'Science'], ascending=[True, True])
print(sorted_df)
Output :
Student_ID English Science Maths SST
4 5 70 82 78 94
1 2 78 85 84 89
0 1 85 90 76 87
3 4 88 91 88 78
2 3 92 78 92 81
```

Group by Function :

The groupby() function in pandas is a powerful tool for grouping data based on some criteria and then performing aggregate functions on each group. It allows you to split a DataFrame into groups based on one or more columns and then apply functions to those groups independently.

The general syntax of the groupby() function is as follows:

DataFrame.groupby(by=None, axis=0, level=None, as_index=True, sort=True, group_keys=True, squeeze=False, observed=False)

Code :

```python
import pandas as pd
```

```python
    # Sample data for 10 students
data = {
'Class': ['A', 'A', 'B', 'B', 'A', 'B', 'A', 'B', 'A', 'B'],
'English': [85, 78, 92, 88, 70, 95, 83, 76, 89, 80],
'Science': [90, 85, 78, 91, 82, 76, 88, 93, 84, 79],
'Maths': [76, 84, 92, 88, 78, 87, 81, 90, 85, 82],
'SST': [87, 89, 81, 78, 94, 85, 90, 76, 83, 88]
}
    # Create a DataFrame
df = pd.DataFrame(data)
    # Grouping by the 'Class' column and computing the mean for each subject
grouped_df = df.groupby('Class').mean()
grouped_df1 = df.groupby('Class').sum()

print(grouped_df,"\n")
print(grouped_df1,"\n")
```

    Output :
    Class English Science Maths SST
A 81.0 85.8 80.8 88.6
B 86.2 83.4 87.8 81.6
    Class English Science Maths SST
A 405 429 404 443
B 431 417 439 408

Reshaping Data:

Reshaping data is a common data manipulation task that involves transforming the layout or structure of a dataset. It typically involves converting data between "wide" and "long" formats or pivoting the data to rearrange rows and columns. Pandas provides several functions to reshape data efficiently. Here are some common reshaping techniques in pandas:

1. pivot(): Pivots the DataFrame from long to wide format, where the unique values of one column become the new column headers, and the data is populated accordingly.

2. melt(): Unpivots the DataFrame from wide to long format, where multiple columns are combined into a single column, and their corresponding values are placed in another column.

3. stack() and unstack(): Stack converts columns to rows, and unstack converts rows back to columns, effectively pivoting data between different levels of a multi-index DataFrame.

4. pivot_table(): Creates a spreadsheet-style pivot table based on DataFrame data, similar to the pivot table functionality in spreadsheet software.

5. stack() and unstack() with multi-index: Used to pivot data when working with hierarchical index levels.

Here's an example to demonstrate reshaping using pivot() and melt()

Code:

```python
import pandas as pd
    # Sample data for 3 students and their marks in two subjects
data = {
'Student': ['Aadil', 'Ruheen', 'Zeenat'],
'Subject1': [85, 78, 92],
'Subject2': [90, 85, 78],
}
```

```
# Create a DataFrame
df = pd.DataFrame(data)
    # Pivot the DataFrame from long to wide format
pivoted_df = df.pivot(index='Student', columns='Subject1', values='Subject2')
    print("Pivoted DataFrame:")
print(pivoted_df)
    # Melt the DataFrame from wide to long format
melted_df = df.melt(id_vars='Student', var_name='Subject', value_name='Marks')
    print("\nMelted DataFrame:")
print(melted_df)
    Output:
    Pivoted DataFrame:
Subject1 78 85 92
Student
Aadil NaN 90.0 NaN
Ruheen 85.0 NaN NaN
Zeenat NaN NaN 78.0
    Melted DataFrame:
Student Subject Marks
0 Aadil Subject1 85
1 Ruheen Subject1 78
2 Zeenat Subject1 92
3 Aadil Subject2 90
4 Ruheen Subject2 85
5 Zeenat Subject2 78
```

In this example, pivot() converts the DataFrame from long to wide format based on the 'Subject1' and 'Subject2' columns. The resulting DataFrame will have 'Subject1' values as new columns and 'Subject2' values as their corresponding values.

On the other hand, melt() unpivots the DataFrame from wide to long format, combining 'Subject1' and 'Subject2' columns into the 'Subject' column and their corresponding values into the 'Marks' column.

These are just some of the basic reshaping techniques in pandas. Depending on your data and analysis requirements, you may need to use other functions like stack(), unstack(), or pivot_table() to achieve the desired data structure.

Checking Missing Values:

In pandas, you can easily check for missing values in a DataFrame using the isnull() and notnull() functions. These functions return a DataFrame or Series of Boolean values, where True indicates the presence of a missing value (NaN or None) and False indicates a non-missing value.

Here are some common methods to check for missing values in pandas:

1. isnull(): Returns a DataFrame of the same shape as the input, where each element is a boolean value indicating whether it is a missing value (True) or not (False).

2. notnull(): Returns the opposite of isnull(), where each element is a boolean value indicating whether it is not a missing value (True) or is a missing value (False).

3. any(): Returns a boolean value for each column or row, indicating whether any missing value exists in that column or row. This is useful to check if the entire DataFrame has missing values.

4. sum(): Returns the count of missing values for each column or row, where True is treated as 1 and False is treated as 0. This gives you the total number of missing values in each column or row.

Code:

```python
import pandas as pd
    # Sample data with missing values
data = {
'A': [1, 2, None, 4, 5],
'B': [6, None, 8, 9, 10],
'C': [11, 12, 13, None, 15]
}
    # Create a DataFrame
df = pd.DataFrame(data)
    # Check for missing values using isnull()
print("Checking for missing values using isnull():")
print(df.isnull())
    # Check for non-missing values using notnull()
print("\nChecking for non-missing values using notnull():")
print(df.notnull())
    # Check if any missing value exists in the DataFrame using any()
print("\nChecking if any missing value exists using any():")
print(df.isnull().any())
    # Count the missing values in each column using sum()
print("\nCount of missing values in each column:")
print(df.isnull().sum())
    # Check if the entire DataFrame has any missing value using any().any()
print("\nChecking if the entire DataFrame has any missing value:")
print(df.isnull().any().any())
```

Output:

Checking for missing values using isnull():

```
A B C
0 False False False
1 False True False
2 True False False
3 False False True
4 False False False
```

Checking for non-missing values using notnull():

```
A B C
0 True True True
1 True False True
2 False True True
3 True True False
4 True True True
```

Checking if any missing value exists using any():

```
A True
B True
C True
dtype: bool
```

Count of missing values in each column:

```
A 1
B 1
```

C 1
dtype: int64
    Checking if the entire DataFrame has any missing value:
True

This will display the Boolean DataFrame with True/False values indicating the presence of missing values in each cell. Additionally, you can use the any() function along with sum() to get an overview of the missing values across columns and rows.

Dropping Missing Values in pandas:

In pandas, you can drop missing values from a DataFrame using the dropna() function. This function allows you to remove rows or columns that contain missing values (NaN or None) based on specified criteria.

Here's the general syntax for the dropna() function:

DataFrame.dropna(axis=0, how='any', thresh=None, subset=None, inplace=False)

Parameters:

axis: Specifies whether to drop rows (axis=0, default) or columns (axis=1) containing missing values.

how: Specifies the criteria for dropping. Possible values are:

'any': Drops rows/columns if it contains any missing value (default).

'all': Drops rows/columns only if all values are missing.

thresh: Specifies the minimum number of non-null values required to keep a row or column.

subset: Specifies a list of column names to consider for dropping. Only the specified columns will be checked for missing values.

inplace: If True, the DataFrame will be modified in place, and the missing values will be dropped directly from the original DataFrame.

Code:

```python
import pandas as pd
    # Sample data with missing values
data = {
'A': [1, 2, None, 4, 5],
'B': [6, None, 8, 9, 10],
'C': [11, 12, 13, None, 15]
}
    # Create a DataFrame
df = pd.DataFrame(data)
print("DataFrame before dropping rows: ")
print(df,"\n")
    # Drop rows containing any missing values
cleaned_df = df.dropna()
    print("\n DataFrame after dropping rows with any missing values:")
print(cleaned_df)
```

    Output:
    DataFrame before dropping rows:
A B C
0 1.0 6.0 11.0
1 2.0 NaN 12.0
2 NaN 8.0 13.0
3 4.0 9.0 NaN
4 5.0 10.0 15.0

DataFrame after dropping rows with any missing values:

A B C

0 1.0 6.0 11.0

4 5.0 10.0 15.0

In this example, the DataFrame df contains missing values in rows 2 and 4. After applying dropna(), those rows are removed, and the resulting DataFrame cleaned_df only contains rows with all non-null values.

You can customize the behavior of dropna() using the optional parameters mentioned above. For instance, you can set how='all' to drop rows or columns only if all values are missing, or use subset to specify a subset of columns to consider for dropping.

Estimating Missing Values in pandas :

In pandas, you can estimate missing values using various techniques to fill in or impute the missing data. Imputing missing values can be beneficial for data analysis and modeling, as it allows you to retain more data for analysis and potentially improve the performance of your models.

Here are some common techniques to estimate missing values in pandas:

1. Using the fillna() method:

1. You can use fillna() to fill missing values with a specific constant, such as zero or the mean, median, or mode of the column.

2. This method allows you to forward-fill (method='ffill') or backward-fill (method='bfill') missing values using the last known value in the column.

You can also specify the limit parameter to limit the number of missing values filled.

2. Using statistical measures:

You can use statistical measures like mean, median, or mode to fill missing values based on the characteristics of the column.

For example, you can use mean() or median() functions to calculate the mean or median of a column and fill missing values with these values.

3. Using interpolation:

The interpolate() method allows you to fill missing values using various interpolation methods, such as linear interpolation, polynomial interpolation, or spline interpolation.

4. Using machine learning-based imputation:

For more advanced imputation techniques, you can use machine learning algorithms, such as K-nearest neighbors (KNN), regression, or matrix factorization methods.

Scikit-learn and other libraries provide implementations of these algorithms that can be used in combination with pandas.

Code:

```python
import pandas as pd
    # Sample data with missing values
data = {
'A': [1, 2, None, 4, 5],
'B': [6, None, 8, 9, 10],
'C': [11, 12, None, None, 15]
}
    # Create a DataFrame
df = pd.DataFrame(data)
print(df,"\n")
    # Fill missing values with the mean of each column
filled_df = df.fillna(df.mean())
```

```
    print("DataFrame after filling missing values with mean:")
print(filled_df,"\n")
    # Interpolate missing values using linear interpolation
interpolated_df = df.interpolate()
    print("\nDataFrame after interpolating missing values:")
print(interpolated_df,"\n")
```

Output:

```
   A B C
0 1.0 6.0 11.0
1 2.0 NaN 12.0
2 NaN 8.0 NaN
3 4.0 9.0 NaN
4 5.0 10.0 15.0
DataFrame after filling missing values with mean:
   A B C
0 1.0 6.00 11.000000
1 2.0 8.25 12.000000
2 3.0 8.00 12.666667
3 4.0 9.00 12.666667
4 5.0 10.00 15.000000
DataFrame after interpolating missing values:
   A B C
0 1.0 6.0 11.0
1 2.0 7.0 12.0
2 3.0 8.0 13.0
3 4.0 9.0 14.0
4 5.0 10.0 15.0
```

ᗞᗞᗞ

SIXTEEN
SOME IMPORTANT PROGRAMS